D0312202

# God
## Allows
## U-Turns®

## for
# teens

TRUE STORIES

# Books by Allison Bottke

*God Allows U-Turns for Teens*
*God Allows U-Turns for Women*

*A Stitch in Time*
*– a novel –*

*I Can't Do It All**

*with Tracie Peterson and Dianne O'Brian

# allison bottke
and Cheryll Hutchings

**God Allows U-Turns**®

TRUE STORIES

## for teens

the choices we make

change the story of our life©

Published by Bethany House Publishers
11400 Hampshire Avenue South
Bloomington, Minnesota 55438

Bethany House Publishers is a division of
Baker Publishing Group, Grand Rapids, Michigan.

Printed in the United States of America

**Library of Congress Cataloging-in-Publication Data**

God allows U-turns for teens : the choices we make change the story of our life / [compiled by] Allison Bottke and Cheryll Hutchings.
    p.  cm.
    Summary: "A book of faith in action for teens—these slice-of-life stories offer a confidence-building look at passionate faith changing, encouraging, inspiring, and healing lives. Perfect for devotional readings"—Provided by publisher.
    ISBN 0-7642-0181-6 (pbk.)
    1. Christian teenagers—Prayer-books and devotions—English. I. Bottke, Allison. II. Hutchings, Cheryll.

BV4850.G58     2006
242'.63—dc22

                                       2005032501

For Christopher
May the Lord continue to guide your U-turn journey of life.
I'm proud of how far you've come. I love you.


For Aaron and Scott
Though we may have had a few bumps along the road,
our trip together through the teen years was on
fairly smooth pavement. Thanks for being such great sons!
Your dad and I are very proud of you
and love you both very much.

# Table of Contents

CHAPTER one: **Choosing to Take a Stand**          **11**

**Free at Last** *by Kitty Chappell*
**A Night With the Band** *by Jennifer Devlin*
**Perfectly Imperfect** *by Candice Killion*
**Special Agent** *by Sydney Tate Williams*
**Traci's Brave Stand** *by Joan Clayton as told by Lane Clayton*
**The Price of Acceptance** *by Cara Symank Parker*
**Extreme Makeover: Life Edition** *by Laura Farrar*
**The Hidden Blessing** *by Ann Eide*
**Fingertip Faith Under Fire** *by Lynette Marie Galisewski*

CHAPTER two: **Choosing to Forgive**          **47**

**Sweet Sixteen** *by Gloria Cassity Stargel as told by Shelly Teems Johnson*
**It's Not Fair!** *by Helen Grace Lescheid as told by Cathy Lescheid*
**Turning Point** *by Amber Renee Medrano*
**When Missy Rejected God** *by Genetta Adair*
**God Forgives** *by Helen Grace Lescheid as told by Susan Houle*

CHAPTER three: **Choosing Love**          **73**

**A Genuine Soldier** *by Gail Dickert*
**First Love** *by Sandra J. Campbell*
**Where There Is Hope** *by Bonnie Scheid*

**If Only I Were Beautiful** *by Amy Nicole Wallace*
**My Daddy's Lap** *by Sharen Watson*
**Bob's About-Face** *by Laura Nixon*
**Through God's Eyes** *by Candace Carteen*

CHAPTER four: **Choosing to Pray**          103

**Giving From the Heart** *by Wendy Dunham*
**Close Encounter** *by Linda Evans Shepherd*
**A Handle on Our Prayers** *by Carol Genengels*
**Winning Is More Than a Score** *by Jeanne Pallos as told by Dave Tepper*

CHAPTER five: **Choosing Life**          119

**Just Trust Me** *by Heather Tomasello*
**Jonny's Gift of Life** *by Ann Jean Czerwinski*
**Beautiful, Beautiful Scars** *by Jan Kern*
**The Truth Will Set You Free** *by Karen Kosman as told by Priscilla Cruz*
**The Story With No Ending** *by D. Marie Hutko*
**Leaving Luggage in France** *by Charles Gibson*
**The Cop That God Sent** *by Karen Kosman*

CHAPTER six: **Choosing to Witness**          147

**Kaleidoscope** *by Joyce Stark*
**Accepting Without Understanding** *by Shelley Wake*
**Just Different Enough** *by Sandra McGarrity*
**Six Months to Live** *by Eva Allen*
**A Casual Witness** *by Esther M. Bailey as told by Matt Lutz*
**The Help-Wanted Ad in the Bible** *by Sharon Dunn*
**A Father's Love** *by Michael T. Powers*

**Boomerang Blessings** *by Esther M. Bailey* *as told by Amber Egelston*
**An Ordinary Kid** *by Rebekah Hamrick*


CHAPTER seven: **Choosing to Triumph**          **175**

**Proud to Be Me** *by Tyrice Harrell*
**First Prize** *by Steven Manchester*
**Yes, Daddy, I Promise** *by Nancy C. Anderson*
**Two Cups** *by Lynn Ludwick*
**Sentence Overturned!** *by Carolyn Byers Ruch* *as told by Benjamin D. Ruch*
**Journal to a Friend** *by Carol Oyanagi*


CHAPTER eight: **Choosing Salvation**          **197**

**Fifteen Months** *by Christy Heitger-Casbon* *as told by Jason Gomez*
**Fire on the Mountain Tonight** *by Laura L. Smith*
**High on Jesus** *by Mary Lee Brown* *as told by Dave*
**Dating God** *by Christy Carlson*
**And a Teen Will Lead Him** *by Nancy B. Gibbs*
**The Day the Cheering Stopped** *by Gloria Cassity Stargel* *as told by John C. Stewart*
**He Lives With Me, But We're Not Married—And Mom Approves!** *by Michele D. Newhouse*
**Two Words That Changed My Life** *by W. Terry Whalin*

CHAPTER **one**

# choosing to take a stand

*David said to Saul, "Let no one lose heart on account of this Philistine; your servant will go and fight him."* —1 Samuel 17:32

When David fought Goliath, he wasn't yet old enough to be in the military, he refused to wear armor, his brother tried to humiliate him, and Goliath was insulted because David was just a kid. Yet David took a stand in front of his big brothers, the army, the king, and an enemy who scared a military force of thousands spitless. He picked up five stones, looked Goliath square in the belly button, and told him, "I'm not only gonna kill you, I'm gonna cut your head off with your own sword!" What a stand he took—and won! Do you have any Goliaths in your life? Can you take a stand in spite of family ridicule and opposition from friends? Can you look your Goliath in the belly button and know you'll be victorious with God's help? Why did David pick up five stones? Tradition says Goliath had four brothers. Yep. Now, that's taking a stand!

# Free at Last

by Kitty Chappell
GILBERT, ARIZONA

The cold, steel muzzle of my father's gun pressed my temple, causing a sharp pain in my head. My heart began to race out of control.

"One of these days I am going to blow your head off," he said in a calculated, convincing tone. "I'm sick and tired of your interfering."

I should have been terrified, but I felt a supernatural peace. No longer did the desire to kill him fill and torment me as it had for years. I thought back over my last four years. . . .

I had just turned fourteen when I started daydreaming about wrestling the gun away from my dad and shooting him. I thought it was the only way to stop him from killing me or anyone else in the house. Consumed and tortured by this thought, I prayed to the God of my maternal grandmother. "If you're as powerful as Granny says, God, why don't you do something?" Shortly after that prayer, someone invited me to church. To my surprise, my father, who said religion was a crutch for weaklings, did not stop me from going.

At church, the minister talked about God's love and how God could be trusted to keep His word when He said, "For God so loved the world that he gave his one and only Son, that whoever believes in him shall not perish but have eternal life." I knew that perish meant die, and I was convinced that my father might kill me.

"The best part of all," the minister explained, "is that it doesn't matter that you feel undeserving. God's love and forgiveness are gifts. Through Christ His Son, God offers love, not judgment, and forgiveness, not condemnation."

I knew a lot about feeling undeserving, unforgiven, and guilty; my dad had made sure of that. I felt like everything terrible he did was my fault. This new promise I heard was my only hope, I thought, bowing my head. As I prayed, God's love filled me. That prayer seemed to change everything.

Dad stopped letting me attend church, but I continued to pray and study the Bible I was given. The Bible taught me to pray for those who hurt me, including Dad. It taught me I should love God, serve Him, and fear no man. I prayed I would get to attend church again. After some time passed, friends invited me to go with them to their church. I was surprised and thanked God when Dad let me go again.

A teacher who was open and honest about spiritual things said, "Life isn't going to be perfect just because we are Christians. We still have to live in a sin-polluted world like everyone else." Though things were not improving at home, I was growing spiritually.

I returned home from church that evening to find Dad beating Mom with his gun. Without thinking, I forced myself between them.

So here I was, about to turn eighteen in a few days, with my earthly father shoving a gun to my head, trusting my heavenly Father with my life. What could I say with a gun pressed to my head that would make a difference? Suddenly aware of the Bible I was clutching, I recalled God's words: "Do not fear, for I am with you . . . I will strengthen you and help you."

I raised my head and stared straight into my father's eyes. My voice steady but soft, I said, "If that's what you want to do, Dad, go ahead and pull the trigger. I am ready to die. I know I will go to

Choosing to Take a Stand

heaven, where you cannot hurt me anymore. But remember this: Someday you will stand before God and be held accountable for your actions." He saw no fear in my eyes, but for the first time I saw a hint of fear in his. He lowered the gun. He never threatened me that way again.

I turned eighteen and made a choice to stay with my family, hoping to help protect them. A year later, my mom, brother, sister, and I fled from our home in Texas. We drove straight through to California; far enough away that we hoped Dad wouldn't find us. But he did.

He started writing letters to Mom begging her to come back, swearing he had changed. After months of struggling on her own, it was easy for Mom to convince herself Dad had changed. By then, I had a job I liked and knew I could never live with my father again.

"Please don't go back, Mom," I begged. "I don't trust him."

Mom agreed to let Dad come and get them during Christmas vacation. Our good-byes seemed as heavy and gray as that foggy morning. Maybe things would work out, I thought. After all, people could change—just look at me. As I tearfully hugged each of them, I couldn't shake the uneasy feeling in the pit of my stomach. This sick feeling heightened when I endured a stiff, cold hug from my father.

My fifteen-year-old brother, Chuck, gave me a quick, intense hug. Holding back tears, he crawled into the backseat and sat staring straight ahead like a zombie. When eleven-year-old Chris hugged me, she whispered, "I don't want to go. I'm afraid."

"I know, sweetheart," I said tearfully. "But remember, I'll be praying for all of you." Her pale, frightened face pressed against the car window, Chris waved in slow motion until Dad's blue Ford disappeared from my sight.

Several nights later I received a phone call in which I learned my mother was in the hospital, not expected to live. While Chuck and Chris lay sleeping in their rooms at the back of the house, Dad had beaten Mother in the head with a hammer and left her for dead. The police found and arrested him the next morning.

Mom survived, but it was over a month before she was well enough to leave the hospital. When Dad finally came to trial, his plea was temporary insanity. Like salt in a wound, the defense falsely accused my mother and me of being prostitutes to better my dad's case. Accusing eyes from every direction in the courtroom glared at us. My anger and bitterness increased with each lie my father spoke during his testimony.

"Please help us, Lord," I prayed over and over as we waited for the verdict. Hours later, Dad was found guilty of premeditated attempted murder. He was sentenced to three and a half years in prison.

After the trial, my siblings and I moved away. Finally, freedom, except I had become a prisoner—a prisoner of bitterness. I loved God. I knew no rational person could blame God for the evil choices people make. But that knowledge did not stop my all-consuming hatred for my dad. As the hate festered, it took the joy out of my life. I did not understand why I felt so old and lifeless at twenty. God's word nudged me toward forgiveness, but I refused.

"Dad doesn't deserve forgiveness!" I argued.

Then God reminded me through His word that I hadn't deserved His forgiveness, either. Even if I wanted to, I felt it was humanly impossible for me to forgive Dad. I remembered something else, too. God took my bitter heart and gave me a new one when I accepted Christ. I felt no fear the time Dad pressed his gun to my head. That certainly seemed humanly impossible, I reasoned. God had helped me so much already; surely He could help me forgive. I wanted with all my heart to obey God, yet I couldn't imagine forgiving the man who brutalized my family. I knew God would never force me to do anything against my will, so I prayed, "Help me, Lord, to want to forgive Dad."

A few months later, a powerful desire to choose to forgive my father suddenly enveloped me. My tears washed away the last remnant of resentment as I whispered to an empty room, "I forgive you, Dad, for everything."

At last I was free. Forever.

# A Night With the Band

by Jennifer Devlin

MADISON, ALABAMA

*Riinnnngggg....* the school bell buzzed through the hall, and immediately all the chairs screeched across the floor, backpacks flew through the air and onto backs, and the school day was finished with a mass of emotions charging down the hallway. I hated my after-school job, although there was no reason to. I was a teenager hating anything that got in the way of what I wanted to do. It was a great job. I made good money for a kid and didn't have to save any of it. I could buy clothes, music, or whatever I wanted. A seventeen-year-old girl's dream . . . money for clothes . . . working with your best friend . . . getting great office experience . . . working with really fun people . . . it was perfect, at least on the surface . . .

"You ready to go, Jen?" shouted my best friend from across the long hall of lockers. "No, but let's go anyway. . . ." my voice trailed as we wandered to the car. We sped off to work and hurried in the door right before the clock would prove that we were late. *Answering phones, filing, and computer work . . . what a thrill. I need something exciting,* I thought to myself. After all, being a teenager was all about having fun, right?

All of a sudden a co-worker of ours who was much older asked with an enticing tone, "So, girls, are you interested in coming over to my apartment this weekend? My boyfriend is in a great rock band, and they're all coming over for some fun . . . you can show up, if you're game . . ."

*Game? Who am I, chicken?* Of course I wanted to go, and of course I wanted this band to think I was cool. The problem was, I

Choosing to Take a Stand

had no idea what she was suggesting. We were good kids who had no idea how to spot bad situations. Well, we were good kids that wanted to be cool, so details weren't a concern. The weekend came, and we were off to the apartment across town.

Standing in front of the door, we looked at each other with a sly grin and knocked. Our parents had no clue what we were about to walk into . . . but then again, neither did we. After all, it was a friend from the office . . . harmless, right?

"Can you believe we are invited to hang out with the band?" I whispered as my friend looked at me.

"Hey, girls, come on in! Meet the guys. . . . Hey, guys, the kids are here—be nice, okay?" The voice of our office mate faded down the hall as she walked back to her chair. Everyone said hi and smiled with crooked smiles. They knew we were new to their type of fun, and they were ready to let us join in with anything they were up to. New girls, that was us. New to a lot more than they realized. Yet somehow they made us feel like instant friends. We were cool in the blink of an eye—or at least that was the impression we got.

But this party was different from any we had ever been to. The music was loud, the lights were dim, and everyone was doing whatever they wanted . . . with whomever they wanted. There were cute guys, so we tried to think it wouldn't be too bad. We figured there would be alcohol, and that would be easy enough to avoid . . . but drugs? *Were people really sharing drugs openly and passing them along to the next person?* We had no clue this is what our co-worker meant when she invited us over. We were clueless indeed. As we sat in that room looking at the people we *thought* were cool, and wanting so badly to be cool ourselves, we stood at the proverbial crossroad. To try or not to try. One time wouldn't hurt, so we were told, but we were kids who were raised on the Word of God, and we knew better. How easily we could have hidden our choice that night, and how easily we could have changed our lives . . . in a tragic way.

Small talk and glancing looks from cute guys was a really tough distraction. Attention is a hard thing to turn away from when you are a teenager, but we were more consumed with the choice that was heading our way. *But the cute guys!* Why couldn't we just get to know them without this room full of choices?

*"Lord, I know what I should do, but I can't do it on my own. I don't want to be laughed at, but I have to get out of here! Get me out of here! Get us out of here!"* I yelled in my mind, with my heart screaming and my thoughts racing.

*So, this is how it happens. This is how people change their lives. One simple moment. One simple choice. This is that moment.* I processed all the thoughts as the "party favor" was passed around and headed my way—and I realized that there was so much more to consider than the handsome façade of an older guy.

*"Lord! Get me out of here!"* I silently screamed . . . *"Give me the strength to walk away . . ."* I yelled in the innermost parts of my mind . . . it seemed like eternity was wrapped in those brief moments, and I guess it could have been. To fall away, or to stand firm . . . this was the choice . . . and I was choosing God. I needed Him to help me stand.

You know, the best thing about best friends is that they know what you are thinking, and lots of the time they are thinking the same thing you are. With a quick glance to my closest friend in the world, we made a silent agreement that would band us together even tighter than we had already been. This is the stuff that makes a friend for life. It was almost as if we silently counted to three, then got up simultaneously, smiled, and said we had to go. We did it! By that time we didn't care what they would say or if they would laugh.

But no one laughed—they just kept partying. They were consumed in their own choice, and they were consumed in the lifestyle they had chosen. We had our choice to make, and we did it. We made the right choice . . . even without our parents there to make us do the right thing. Before we could even get out the door, the guys that thought we were so cute one moment were off to the next girl who sat alone. It was such an obvious display of what we could have fallen for. We didn't matter to them at all.

We could have been cool to people that would never matter to us either, but instead we backed our car out of the parking spot, turned onto the road, and headed home. You could have heard a pin drop as we drove in silence for miles. Processing. Thanking God in our hearts. Knowing we had just hit a moment in time we would never forget. Knowing that we had to face that same girl on Monday. Knowing God had given us this moment together, so the choice that had to be made was not made alone, or only in a room full of "cool" people. Knowing the true meaning of sticking together, through thick or thin. The office job may not have been perfect, but our choice was!

# Perfectly Imperfect

by Candice Killion

DAVIE, FLORIDA

When you're overweight in high school, you have some choices to make if you want to survive. You can permit your self-consciousness to permeate everything, making you a loner, a loser, and the brunt of jokes. Or you can be the one *making* the jokes before they have a chance to get to you. I chose the latter.

People in recovery have a saying: "Fake it 'til you make it." It became my mantra. I plastered on a giant smile even when it wasn't really appropriate, cracked sarcastic comments from the back of the classroom, and kept everyone in stitches. Before long, and to my surprise, I wasn't only just treading water and surviving in the high school shark pool—I was actually popular!

I still felt out of place inside, as I shopped with my friends from the cool crowd and they picked out cute, tiny clothes. But they didn't make a big deal out of my size. In fact, they laughed almost as hard as I did when I would pick up a top I couldn't get my left arm into and pretend it was a sausage casing. When I was alone, I went back to the fat girls' department and bought what fit me.

I joined the choir, the pep squad, and the school newspaper. I ran for student council and won. Often I took a deep breath and stopped to survey the state of my performance. If they only knew how I really felt inside! What would happen if I dropped the comedy act? I didn't want to think about it. It was what I perfected and what they expected. Without it, I was just another fat kid sitting miserably in the corner. Just me, and not nearly good enough.

By the time I was a senior, I was the co-editor of the yearbook and had a lot on my social plate, more than I ever dreamed and none of which I wanted to lose. Being an upperclassman had also given me a big head. It was around then that my defensive humor took a different turn. I started targeting other people and their weaknesses: skinny legs, crooked teeth, body odor. And my "friends" laughed even harder than before. Most of them, anyway.

Quietly, stealthily, almost invisibly, a girl who'd been a friend of mine all the way through school began ducking me in the hallways and stopped returning phone calls at home.

"Hey, where have you been hiding?" I cornered her at her locker one afternoon after choir practice. No one else was around.

She drew in a deep breath and looked at me in a way she'd never done before. She looked disgusted, just the way I sometimes thought people who didn't know me reacted to my flabby arms and too-wide rump. Only, she wasn't looking at my body. She was looking into my eyes, where my soul is supposed to be.

"Look," she began, "I don't know if this is a good idea."

"What are you talking about?" I was clueless.

"You're changing." She blurted it out. "And it ain't pretty. That new girl with the big nose? She heard you. I saw her crying. It just isn't right, that's all." She slammed the locker door and walked away.

I went home that night and took a good look at myself in the mirror. When had I forgotten how it felt to be different? Had I, ever? And what gave me the right to point out the inadequacies of others, to sacrifice them so I could continue to feel good about myself?

I looked into my own eyes, into my own soul. I took a good, long look and finally saw myself the way I really was, the way the

Lord made me. Imperfect, like everyone else, but all of us in it together, perfect in His eyes.

I learned how to be serious that night, and how to apologize.

In the days that followed, I also learned what it was like to laugh—a real, full, happy, and unfettered laugh—one that comes from the deepest part of the soul God made, the part that has always been there beneath my fear of not being good enough.

# Special Agent

by Sydney Tate Williams

SIKESTON, MISSOURI

He wasn't dressed like a special agent. He had on a white T-shirt, old washed-out Wrangler jeans, and his favorite cowboy boots. I'm sure the students, teachers, and the principal were expecting a suit and tie. I knew he had probably driven straight to the school from the barn where he kept Cowboy, his team-roping horse. My dad's passion for rodeos was almost as great as his passion for his job.

It was career day at our high school and my dad was one of the speakers. I watched with pride as he walked to the front of the platform to stand at the podium. The three big, black, bold letters on the front of his white T-shirt proclaimed why he was there: FBI. A hush came over the audience when he began to speak.

My dad has been a special agent for the FBI for as long as I can remember, so I've heard all of his stories many times. I knew he would talk about the importance of never giving up your dreams, and how each and every one of us shape the hearts and lives of our loved ones, for better or worse, with our choices. Like I said, I had heard it all before. But the message my dad left with the audience that day will stay with me forever.

Jordi, my best friend, was sitting next to me. She reached out and squeezed my hand when Dad talked about the aftermath of September 11.

I shivered as he described the scene at Ground Zero when he saw it just a few weeks after the terrorist attack. He told stories of how he saw heroism redefined. Dad talked about the healing power of unity as he saw people come together in the dark days following the tragic event. I saw a few teachers dab at their eyes while Dad was talking, and I held my breath, afraid he was going to say something about church or God. I'd heard him tell Mom that morning that the principal had asked him to refrain from mentioning his religious beliefs, but my dad is a dedicated Christian and I knew that would be difficult for him to do.

Like all Americans, September 11, 2001, is a day I will never forget. I had an early dentist appointment that Tuesday morning and was not going to school until after lunch. Mom and I were in the kitchen and had the TV on. I remember watching in horror as the Twin Towers collapsed. Clouds of smoke were billowing skyward as people ran for their lives. It was like a scene from a science-fiction movie. I started crying and my entire body was shaking. Mom held me and we cried together for the next hour, listening to the tragic reports, praying Daddy would call and let us know he was all right. When we finally did hear from him, he told us to pray. He reminded us God loves us and He hears the prayers of those whose suffering seems unbearable. Dad's reassuring words were like a big hug.

When Dad told his audience that he would wrap up his speech with the words of Robert F. Kennedy, I looked over at our principal and saw the smile of relief on his face. I guess he had been worried Dad would end his message with a prayer, too.

"Acts of courage shape human history. Each time a man stands up for an ideal, or acts to improve the lots of others, or strikes out against injustice, he sends forth a tiny ripple of hope."

He paused for a second and then continued. "I am proud to be a special agent for the Federal Bureau of Investigation. After the tragedies of September 11, the world changed. I choose to wear the badge of a special agent because I know we can make a difference. We stand for ideals that strike out against injustice."

I watched as Dad pointed to the three big, black, bold letters on his T-shirt. "I am proud of the bold letters on my shirt. I choose to wear it so others will understand there is an answer. An answer that gives us acts of courage that can shape human history, improve the lots of others, and offer hope."

Dad turned and shook hands with our principal. While the audience politely applauded he walked off the platform and began shaking hands with the students and teachers in the auditorium. Every time Dad shook hands with someone, the applause got louder. People began to stand and the clapping grew louder and louder. By the time he got to the row of seats where I was sitting, the applause was thunderous. I reached out to hug him and he winked at me. That was when I saw the message on his T-shirt. It said *Firm Believer In Christ*.

My dad is a special agent for the FBI, but even more important, my dad is a special agent for God. I am so proud of him.

# Traci's Brave Stand

by Joan Clayton as told by Lane Clayton

PORTALES, NEW MEXICO

"Mom, they did it again." Traci threw her books down and collapsed on the couch, crying her heart out. "They make fun of me. They mock me and laugh."

"Honey, I'm so sorry. It'll be all right. Just because you don't agree with them doesn't make them right and you wrong. You're taking a stand for Jesus and you'll be rewarded for it. Just wait and see."

Traci and her Mom prayed every night: "Dear God, please give me the strength and courage to stand up for you. I don't care what others think, even if it hurts."

Traci's friends liked a pop female music group whose standards did not exactly fit proper role models. Traci stood her ground. She thought the group did not exhibit good examples and voiced her opinion without reservation. Her friends stopped having anything to do with her, criticizing her openly for not liking the trio.

Despite the ridicule and persecution, Traci stood firm. Since the hurt and rejection of her best friend wounded Traci's spirit with agonizing heartache, Traci decided to write Nancy a heart-to-heart letter explaining her position and why. Nancy had been in the same Sunday school class at church.

*Dear Nancy, I want you to be my friend again. I'm sorry if I have done anything to hurt you, but I keep remembering what we learned in Sunday school, to do the right thing whether everybody else does or not. Please be my friend again. Traci.*

"Oh, Traci," Nancy cried over the phone the next day, "I really don't like that group either, but I didn't want to go through what you've gone through. I didn't want to be made fun of or laughed at. I'm so sorry. Yes, I would love to be your friend again, and I want to do the right thing even if everybody else doesn't."

Traci's influence had prevailed. Over the next few weeks, Traci's friends came around and agreed with her. Traci's family was very proud!

"You see, honey, God always wins," her father said. "I just want you to know how proud I am of you." He gave her a big bear hug.

Traci learned a monumental lesson. Yes, persecution will come when a stand is taken for righteousness, but God is faithful. She learned God not only answers prayer, but grants the desires of our hearts, too. Traci's desire had been to have a contemporary radio station in her town that would have singers who were good role models.

One day while visiting at Nancy's house, Traci told Nancy's father, who owned the local radio station, about the need for a contemporary Christian music radio station in their town. You guessed it. There is now a Christian radio station there.

"Delight yourself in the Lord and he will give you the desires of your heart" (Psalm 37:4).

Traci is quite a teenager. She chooses to use her unique gifts of strength and boldness to contribute to the spiritual health of her classmates. She did not let the abandonment of her friends deter her. Her assurance gave her the courage and hope to stand firm for Jesus no matter how difficult the situation.

Traci, once persecuted for her beliefs, now listens with all of her friends to Christian radio, praising the Lord with song and dance.

# The Price of Acceptance

by Cara Symank Parker

ABILENE, TEXAS

Have you ever felt like you just don't quite fit in? I have. I grew up in a Christian home and attended a Christian school through high school—though I never found my place there. It became hardest when I outwardly disagreed with the actions that my peers were involved in. Even in, and maybe especially in, a Christian school, a lot of people don't want to be identified as "Christian." They do everything they can to *not* be Christian. I was ridiculed for not participating with "the crowd." I believed in what the school and the Bible said.

As time went by, I became frustrated, desperately wanting to be part of the group. Tired of fighting the crowd, I let my guard down and decided to join them. I decided it was my only way to be accepted. Each time I would do something I knew was wrong, I would feel guilty and considered pulling away from the group. However, no matter how bad I felt, it was hard to break away. I was feeling accepted—an acceptance I had not felt before I joined "the crowd." For the rest of my high school years, I chose "the crowd's" way over God's way.

On Thanksgiving night of 2001, at the age of nineteen, my entire life was forever changed. Nothing in life had prepared me for what was about to take place. As my family and I prepared to leave my grandparents' house, my mother was standing in the driveway loading up our family's vehicle. My father, my two younger sisters, and I watched in horror as my mother's life was taken away with all

Choosing to Take a Stand

of us looking on. She was hit and killed right there in the driveway by a drunk teenage driver.

That night, in the midst of all the chaos and intense emotional pain, I focused on my mother's teachings to me. Her message about God's grace and love were always made very clear. I knew I had to fully rely on God in order to make it through the gut-retching tragedy.

After the accident, I never returned back to the things I had participated in before in order to gain acceptance. I had a devastating and tragic view of the heartache and pain excessive alcohol use could potentially cause to others. I regret it took something that huge to make me realize the value of life is not based on what my peers think of me or expect of me.

A teenage girl very close to my age killed my mother. I wonder if she felt she needed to "feel worthy" of the crowd she was with. It was at that point God allowed me the choice to make a U-turn in my life. Through Him I gained the courage to stand up to what I knew was right. I was able to talk to the people I had previously wanted acceptance from and tell them I disagreed with their actions. I could tell them their actions were not only wrong, but deadly. I was able to show them how, with God's acceptance, they could turn their lives around.

God has given me unbelievable strength to make it through the loss of my mother. Although I miss her deeply, God has given me a sense of peace. If I were still focused on needing the acceptance of my peers, I would not have the peace I have now. I am currently in college and the majority of the people in my classes share much of the same views as the ones I knew in high school. The difference is

I am now able to stand up for my belief in Christ. I do not have to participate in stuff I know is wrong in order to feel acceptance. Christ has given me the ultimate acceptance I need. Is it going to take a tragedy in your life, like it did for me, in order for you to realize that only God's acceptance matters? I wonder, and so I ask.

# Extreme Makeover: Life Edition

by Laura Farrar

PINOLE, CALIFORNIA

"God, I'm so sick of being alone! Why can't I talk to people?"

Those tearful words seemed to be coming out of my mouth too often. I was only fifteen, and social conversations left me out in the cold. I was so shy. I had never fit in well with my peers. Youth group became torture. I was a wallflower . . . and I was stuck in an endless circle of tears.

While all the girls ignored me, I stood there suffering with rejection, loneliness, bitterness, and depression. I found it easier to turn away from God than to face the problem.

Then came the day I had my first breakdown. It felt like life was just not worth living. But God had another plan. I went to youth group one night where my pastor, Ted, asked, "Are you really okay?"

"I don't know anymore."

"Let's talk."

I described how being shy and lonely was breaking my heart. How being alone had sent me spiraling emotionally. I was just so tired of being alone.

"Laura, I'm going to make a bold proposition. Are you ready to hear this?"

I swallowed and nodded.

"You've memorized Bible verses since you were a little girl. Now you're gonna have to put them to work. I want you to step out on the water in faith and walk. Either you can do all things through Christ . . . or God's a liar."

God a liar? I gulped. Walk on water? What does that mean?

"Let me ask you . . . why don't you talk to people?" Pastor Ted asked.

"I . . . it's like I just . . . can't. I can't get myself to start conversations."

"Next week, I want you to go up to someone and compliment them. Ask them where they got their shoes. Ask them questions."

As he spoke I took note of all his suggestions and examples. I could do this! In my heart I changed my attitude toward people. Suddenly I was dying to talk. For the first time in my life I wanted to run up to people and speak.

Ted continued, "I think you need an extreme makeover. You need to make some major changes in your life. I know you can do this."

And so I did. My extreme makeover has covered my entire life: My room, my attitude, my wardrobe, my shoes, my interests, my makeup, and even my hair. In fact, I cut my waist-length hair eight inches. I wanted to make outside changes to help me feel better.

But the biggest makeover was inside my heart. The next Tuesday night I decided to take the initiative and talk. I was going to make friends! I grabbed several verses and recited them to myself constantly. *I can do all things through Christ who gives me strength. I can do all things . . .* With a deep breath I walked up to Heather, who was sitting by herself. "Hi! What's up?" I said.

The conversation was short, but a success in my world! For me, talking first goes against all I've ever believed. Caution and reducing risks had been important. No more! I can face risking personal rejection because Jesus is holding me up. He gives me courage, strength, and words.

My life made a U-turn when I chose to give up my struggles to God and began to trust in His power. If He can take a shy girl like me and make me more outgoing through His power, I know He can do it for you. Trust Him for your extreme makeover. I did and am I grateful!

# The Hidden Blessing

by Ann Eide

COLUMBUS, MISSISSIPPI

Many years ago, while sitting at a youth convention, I looked at a brochure and wondered what classes my fellow roommates would join. I glanced over to see notes scrawled in the center of one of my roommates' pamphlet: "Meet me at the water fountain at 10:15 A.M." It was a clear indication someone was going to skip the informal introduction ceremony and probably miss several if not all the sessions. Unfortunately, this practice of clowning around was commonplace for some of the kids.

The day's events ended promptly at 4:00 P.M., and our group met at the van. On the ride to our motel, several girls giggled as they discussed plans for that evening. I hauled my bags to my room and tried to settle into the cramped living quarters. To my dismay, I was met by three girls whom I was not in good favor with. "You know, we would love to share the room with Cynthia if you don't mind. And since you are special like Becca, we know you won't mind moving into her room."

The point was, I did mind. After all, they really had no right to group me in the same category as Becca. I did not have cognitive delays, and anyone's guess would deem me normal. Perhaps it was because I came from an overly protective family who wanted to know everything about their kids' activities right from the start. So I was mad and distraught about my being called "special."

It was then that I pondered Becca's predicament. Few people spoke to her. Sadly, Becca would sit and try to smile so as not to act disappointed by the rudeness of her peers. She had been born with a seizure disorder and had developmental delays to some extent. She had not chosen this life, but it was hers all the same.

As I looked at the girls who were pointing and laughing at Becca, I made a choice right then and there. I made the choice to cover Becca with my wing as a mother bird protects her young. Gathering my belongings, I looked up at Cynthia. "Enjoy your stay. I am sure the four of you will have fun together." I threw the key on the bed and walked out politely. Two doors down, I knocked on the door. "Becca, are you there? I've decided to bunk with you." The door opened without hesitation, and there in the doorway stood a most happy girl.

Upon settling in, Becca and I walked across the street to get something to eat. As luck would have it, we ran into our youth group. The casual hellos were exchanged and we found a table near our group. "So tell me, Becca, what groups are you interested in going to tomorrow?" She unfolded her pamphlet and scanned the list. "I'd like to go to the sign language and music session, Bible Study for Beginners, and the Crafts for Christ workshop." Her eyes sparkled with enthusiasm as I agreed to participate in all three of her choices. Becca wrote notes as we continued to discuss what other workshops were available for Friday and Saturday.

After dinner was over, we retired back to our room. It was a small room, with a table and two chairs, a television, and two double beds. Becca brought a deck of cards and we played easy games like Go Fish and War until almost 10:00 P.M. I sat back on the bed with my Bible in hand and Becca asked, "Why do you think I was made special?"

I shrugged my shoulders and smiled. "I don't know why, Becca, but God knows. We never really know what He has in store for us. We just have to trust God."

Becca smiled. "I guess you're right. Well, good night, I'll see you in the morning, bright and early."

That night I began thinking about all the day's events. I really wanted to be included in the other activities with my peers, but my gut kept saying to let it go. I didn't want to leave Becca alone. Just because she may be behind in learning, she still needed friends. I prayed to God I would make wise choices. I fell asleep with Bible in hand and awoke to daylight and Becca singing with the radio.

"Morning sleepyhead," Becca greeted.

I glanced at the clock, which read 6:45. "No one gets up this early. Good night."

Becca was relentless as she pulled the covers off of the bed and took away my pillow. "Get up! Van leaves at 8:00 A.M. and I'm hungry. Let's get something to eat!"

Groggy, I sat up on the edge of the bed. "Okay, fine. Give me fifteen minutes and I'll go with you to the café." As I got dressed, I had a feeling this was going to be a long day.

"Coffee?" the young waitress asked.

"Uh, Coca-Cola and a doughnut. What about you, Becca? What do you want?"

Becca glanced at the menu and replied, "I'll have an omelet and orange juice." She then turned her attention toward me and seemed to hang on my every word.

"Pardon me. I'm not a morning person. I wish I had three more hours of sleep," I said, trying to hold back a yawn.

"I slept good. I can't wait to go to the workshops! I'm excited!

Are you?" she asked. I nodded sleepily.

The van pulled up and we were off to the convention center. At the first session, I could barely keep my eyes open. Too many happy, peppy voices, I thought.

Becca handed me a piece of paper and a pen. "Could you write down the notes with me?"

I nodded, but the first lecture was boring and I mainly dabbled on the paper. Becca looked disappointed as she saw I had inadvertently written the word *boring* in big letters.

"You aren't having fun, are you? I'm sorry. Maybe you should go back to your friends."

I smiled. "I'm sleepy, that's all. Let's get to the next session. We don't want to be late." I gathered our materials and we raced down the corridor to the next workshop.

As the day progressed, the workshops did have a good measure of interest and fun incorporated in them. I remembered how the note made Becca feel, and I promised God I would do my part to be more aware of her feelings. The next two days went without a hitch. There were lots of entertaining activities and free time to enjoy outside the events.

Saturday afternoon our whole group got together and discussed a variety of workshops, both good and bad. Some kids had nothing to say at all, while others shared what materials they had picked up along the way. We ended the group time by sharing what the trip had meant to each of us. Becca said she had a fun time with the sign language workshop, and I agreed. I heard snickers from the same four girls who earlier had classified me as "special."

But this time I said, "Perhaps you would have enjoyed it if you had gone, too."

The group ended in prayer and we raced to pack our belongings for the trip home. The ride home was uneventful, quiet and dark. The driver had driven all night long and we arrived at the church parking lot at sunup. Wearily I said my good-byes as I hopped into my mom's car and headed home. From that point onward, Becca would always sit beside me at youth group functions, and I didn't mind.

Many years passed, and one day while visiting a bookstore, I saw Becca. I walked up and hugged her.

"Becca, how are you?"

The same smile from years before flashed across her face. "I'm good. I work here now. How are you?"

"Things are going well. How about helping me find a book for my preschooler?"

Becca replied, "Right this way." She paused and put her hand on my shoulder. "You know, my best memory of the youth group is when we shared a room together at the convention. How you chose me instead of those girls. I had the best time going everywhere with you."

I smiled. "I had fun, too."

What was thought of as a bad experience took on a different form that March day. It took Becca ten seconds to reveal the convention was a hidden blessing for both of us. God knew exactly what He had in store for us in that divine appointment that changed our lives. What an awesome convention it was!

# Fingertip Faith Under Fire

by Lynette Marie Galisewski

LITTLETON, COLORADO

"Show me evidence of God in this world! Show me someone who's better for believing in a higher power . . . for abdicating the control of their life to someone else who supposedly cares from a remote heaven. Did any one of you talk to God today?" Miss Woodward, my sophomore-class English teacher, asked us as we cowered in our seats.

I nervously fidgeted with the cross hanging conspicuously from my neck, trying to decide whether to tuck it into a less obvious spot under my collar. Fearing a movement of my hand might draw her attention, and thus her wrath, I held my position, forced to feel the crossbars of my so-called faith in my fingertips. It was a moment of reckoning. I felt a kinship with Shadrach, Meshach, and Abednego as the trumpets heralded their fiery call to take a stand for their convictions. When King Nebuchadnezzar commanded all to bow down to the golden god and worship it, these three defied him and refused to worship any other god except their own. When thrown into the fiery furnace, the Lord saved them. The only problem was I wasn't them!

If I hadn't talked to God already that day, I sure was now! *No, God, not me . . . not now! I'm a wimp . . . I've always been a wimp . . . and always will be! I'm not the one to speak up for you. I barely know you myself! We've kind of lost contact over these past few years. I'm still kinda mad at you for giving me this disgustingly curly hair, and not causing anyone to ask me to the homecoming dance!*

How I wished I had taken my friend Ellen's advice on the first day of school last fall. The minute she saw Miss Woodward's name on my schedule of classes, she groaned. "Oh no, Lynette! You got Miss Woodward for English! Not only will you be stuck with all the brains in the school, but she's an absolute witch! She takes pleasure in putting you in a meat grinder and eating you alive! Get out while you can!"

Nature and nurture had equipped me well to be an appeaser. My personality was naturally shy and introverted, and the fact my dad's work got us transferred every one to two years taught me how to adapt to new school environments with the least amount of outward pain. I had confidence Miss Woodward's class would be no different.

How wrong I was! How costly that miscalculation!

My first week in class only validated Ellen's prophetic warning. Boot camp never stripped anyone of their identity and self-confidence more than Miss Woodward's "educational techniques." Intimidation, coercion, and ridicule were her bywords. She even prided herself in perfecting them. No one was exempt. Not even polished placators like me. From day one she began dismantling my survival mechanisms.

"Miss Northrup, you're looking especially intelligent today," Miss Woodward taunted. "Tell us what is wrong with Mr. Johnson's line of reasoning in his interpretation of the protagonist's role in *Fahrenheit 451*."

"Ahh, er," I stammered, trying to jump-start my brain. I barely understood what a protagonist was, much less had the knowledge to critique someone else's opinion about a book that made no sense to me.

"Those are filler words for an empty brain, Miss Northrup," she bellowed. "Your paper showed equal vacuity."

The class broke into a nervous laugh . . . both as an effort to slice through the tension as well as an expression of relief since they weren't the one presently sizzling on the hot seat. I couldn't blame them. I had probably issued similar sounds during another classmate's misery.

Actually, this was probably part of Miss Woodward's strategy. She stripped us of the strength we could draw from our shared suffering. So we suffered alone.

I can't say for sure if this was everyone's experience, but being a shy, sensitive person, everybody's skinning was my own skinning. I died a slow death with each cutting word.

"Mr. Garcia, how did you ever get into tenth grade, much less this honors' class?" hacked Miss Woodward's butcherous tongue. "You obviously have no idea what a preposition is and where it should go! Here is a third-grade reader to refresh your memory."

The thin-skinned were effaced to no skin. I was naked, vulnerable, and whimpering as inconspicuously as I could under Miss Woodward's weak-seeking surveillance. Like a wounded animal trying to hide my limp from a hyena circling the herd, I pulled out all of my best blending techniques.

A few years before Miss Woodward stormed into my world, I had unwillingly been swallowed up by the tornado of adolescence. The turmoil inside had dulled my childhood ear to any sense of God's love for me. He had been feeling like a stranger to me for some time. Most of my prayers centered around begging and bargaining with God to magically erase the pimples from my face or give me a new outfit to make me popular with my peers. It was the best I could muster up given my inner confusion and neediness. Still pimple-clad and dressed in hand-me-downs, my faith was faltering and I was clinging on by my fingertips—literally.

At this moment, feeling the cross pressed secretly in the grip of my fingers, I knew it was now or never . . . and given the ferocity of my present opponent, *never* was looking pretty good.

The mocking challenge still hung in the air. "Did any of you talk to God today?"

Why was time standing still? Why was there a burning in my heart? Why did this tiny cross concealed in my hand feel like the most important thing in the entire world? Suddenly, Jesus hanging on it, in the midst of His own storm of ridicule, caused something to well up inside of me way beyond anything I could have conjured up on my own.

The inner tension burst like a pressure cooker in full whistle. I dropped my fingertip cover, exposing my cross, and raised my trembling but determined hand. "Yes, Miss Woodward," I volunteered out loud. "I talked to God today . . . and He makes a difference in my life."

That's all I said. Not very profound. Inwardly I braced myself for the guillotine to fall, but outwardly I maintained my calm air of certainty. There was no *er-ahh*ing out of this stance. I had beacon-lighted myself out of the safety of the crowd.

Like two cats stuck in a hair-raised standoff, Miss Woodward and I locked our stares and played chicken with our eyes. Eternity seemed to come and stay until she broke the stare with these very unexpected words.

"Miss Northrup, thank you for believing in your God enough to take a stand. Let that be a lesson to all of us. Class dismissed."

I was dumbfounded. I'm not sure how I made it out of the classroom that day, or how anyone else did, for that matter. We were dazed by the outcome. Someone had gone head-to-head with Miss Woodward and was alive to talk about it! Having witnessed my mealy-mouthed sputtering in the past, my classmates were all the more confounded.

"How did she ever pull that one off?" I overheard someone whisper as we staggered out the door.

I wanted to cry out it really hadn't been me . . . something inside of me had staged a coup over my will. I was as baffled as anyone by the whole ordeal . . . not only by Miss Woodward's affirming response, but even more by having tapped into something inside of me . . . so powerful, so unlike me . . . so courageously convicted!

I laid the cross carefully on the outside of my shirt, feeling a strange sense of pride. It was no longer just an ornament. It was a statement . . . a statement of my deepest beliefs. Somehow the pimples on my face and the hand-me-down clothes faded in their importance. God had made himself real to me and I felt His power surge in and through me!

The choice to make a stand for my faith in God changed my relationship with Him forever.

*A postscript.* At a high school reunion ten years later, I heard Miss Woodward had gotten married and had a baby girl. She had chosen to have her baptized in a Christian church! I'd like to think in our moment of locked stares, Miss Woodward encountered genuine faith . . . the kind that transforms shy, fearful unlikelies into courageous people of conviction. I owe her two big thank-you's: one for teaching me how to think and write (as painful as it was), and the other for forcing me to find my faith in the blaze of her fiery furnace.

# choosing to forgive

*Do not judge, and you will not be judged. Do not condemn, and you will not be condemned. Forgive, and you will be forgiven.* —Luke 6:37

Remember that red crayon? You were five and it looked so new. It called your name. But Klepto, who also swiped the last red chair at your table, grabbed it first. So you took it back, right out of his hand. And he tattled to the teacher. Bet the teacher made you say sorry— remember that? Or maybe you were the kid who had to hear that meaningless sorry. Been there, done that? I doubt that sorry situation was what Jesus meant when He said to forgive. And since then, there's been a lot of other stuff—big, bad, brutal stuff—that makes *sorry* more meaningless. Like when your mother slapped you. Or your dad abandoned you. Chances are the person who hurt you the deepest may never even say sorry. But can you forgive anyway? Can you break free of the chain binding you to the one who's scarred you? It's hard. Impossible, in fact, without Jesus' help. But His scars prove He has forgiven us. And He will help us get past our scars to forgiveness.

# Sweet Sixteen

by Gloria Cassity Stargel as told by Shelly Teems Johnson

GAINESVILLE, GEORGIA

"Hurry and get dressed, Shelly," Mom's overly cheerful voice penetrated the closed door to my room. "The sun's shining. Let's go riding!"

Mom knew I was on the phone with my boyfriend. The last thing I wanted to do on that Sunday afternoon was ride horses with my mother. Yet I dared not argue back, not after our blowup the night before.

*I'm sixteen years old, for crying out loud!* I seethed. *Why can't she just stay out of my life?*

Sometimes I *hated* my mother. I desperately wanted her to give me more space. She sponsored my cheerleading squad. She attended every one of my volleyball and softball games. She even taught at my school. Wherever I went, she was there! As if that were not bad enough, she always ordered me around. Even my friends noticed.

When I was little I *liked* it when Mom was protective, when she got involved in my activities. But now I wanted independence and the chance to make my own mistakes.

Truth is, in spite of Mom's constant surveillance, I managed to break most of the rules at our private Christian school. The more I rebelled, the more Mom clamped down. The more she clamped down, the more I rebelled.

Take the night before when we had the blowup. So I was a few minutes late coming in. Well, maybe it was more like an hour late. Just as I expected, Mom followed me into my room.

"Where were you all this time, Shelly?" she quizzed. "I worry about you when you're late. *Anything* could have happened! Why didn't you call me?" On and on and on.

As usual, Mom threw in a little Scripture for good measure, as if she didn't drill me on memory verses at our breakfast table *every morning of my life!*

"Remember, Shelly," she'd said that night, "the Bible says, 'Children, obey your parents. . . . Honor your father and mother that it may go well with you and that you may enjoy long life on the earth.'" Then she added, "Shelly, your life just shortened by one day!"

"Mom," I yelled, "will you just leave me alone?" When she finally left, I slammed the door behind her.

Today she was pretending nothing had happened, trying to make us look like the ideal loving family of her dreams. Meantime, after hanging up the telephone, I sat thinking, *What is all this horseback-riding business? Mom isn't even a horse person! She just wants to know what I'm doing every minute.*

Halfheartedly, I pulled on my riding boots, then slugged over to the dresser. Reaching for a comb, my hand brushed against the necklace Mom had given me for my last birthday. *I'd better wear this or she'll ask where it is.* Reluctantly, I fastened the silver chain around my neck and straightened the pendant—the silver outline of a heart with its message, in script, suspended inside: Sweet Sixteen. *Yeah, sure, Mom.*

By the time I got to the barn, Dad had already saddled Miss Char-Deck—we usually called her Charcey. Mom was swinging into the saddle.

Choosing to Forgive

"Mom, what are you doing?" I shrieked. "You've never ridden Charcey before! She's a *big* horse."

*I cannot believe this woman!* I thought. *She'll do anything to be part of my life. And I just want her out of it!*

While Dad was bridling the Arabian named Babe, Mom discovered her stirrups were too long. Before Dad could turn around to adjust them, Charcey charged away at full gallop. *What has gotten into Charcey?*

Scared and inexperienced, Mom probably reacted by doing all the wrong things. Whatever the reason, Charcey was out of control. Never had I seen her run so fast, her mane and tail flying in the wind! It was as though she had to show off what a quarter horse is bred to do: win short-distance races. With every stride of her powerful haunches, she gained speed.

I watched, horrified, as Charcey's hooves beat at the earth, faster and faster—like something possessed, a thousand pounds of straining muscle thundering across the pasture.

With lightning speed, Charcey reached a corner of the pasture fence—a place of decision. Should she jump? *No. Too high with a ditch on the other side.* Other choice? *Make a ninety-degree turn.* Charcey turned. Mom flew high into the air, crashed through a barbed-wire fence, and landed on the sun-parched ground.

THUD!

Then—*nothing.* Except for Charcey's hoofbeats as she tore back to the barn.

*Dear God! No! No! This can't be happening!* I sprinted across the pasture.

"Mom! Mom!" *Please, God, don't let her be dead! I didn't mean it,*

*God. I don't really want her out of my life! Please!*

The barbed wire held her in an almost kneeling position. Her right wrist and hand dangled the wrong way, her neck and head were turned as if broken. Blood oozed from gashes on her back. *Is she breathing? Please, God, she thinks I don't love her!*

"Mom?"

After what seemed an eternity, I heard a moan—then a weak, "I'm okay, Shelly."

"Mom! Oh, Mom! I didn't mean to be so hateful. I *do* love you, Mom." I carefully and gently untangled her hair from the barbed wire. I barely was able to see through my tears.

"Oh, Mama, I'm so sorry. I'm so sorry."

"I know, Shelly," Mom somehow managed while I made one last tug on her shredded pink sweater and freed her from the wire.

"We have to get you to the hospital," Dad said, jumping back astride Babe and turning her toward the barn. "I'll call an ambulance."

"No," Mom said. Because she was a nurse, we listened. "You can carry me to the van, then drive me to the hospital."

Dad barreled down the highway, all the while trying to raise a police escort on the two-way radio. Meanwhile, I did what Mom had taught me: I quoted Scripture.

"'Rejoice in the Lord always,'" I said, close to her ear, "'and again I say rejoice.'"

For once I must have done the right thing, because Mom, through all her pain, started quoting Scripture, one verse after another, all the way to the hospital.

She spent most of the next three months in a wheelchair, and during that time we did a lot of talking.

"Mom," I told her, "I know I act a lot like Charcey did the day of your accident. I just want to charge through life without being held back, not missing anything."

"Yes, Shelly, and I always want to be in control, to make sure things go right. To protect you from getting hurt."

We decided because we were so different, we'd probably always clash over one thing or another. We agreed on something else, too. We loved each other, no matter what.

Still, I felt a need to do something more to make things right. One day at school I asked permission to speak at our chapel service. Standing on stage behind the microphone, I took a deep breath as I addressed the other students, the faculty, and especially Mom, who sat in the back of the room in her wheelchair.

"I want to apologize for all the mistakes I've made this year, mistakes that have hurt others," I confessed. "Worst of all, they hurt my mom."

I confessed how hateful I had been to my mother. How I yelled at her to stay out of my life. Then I described Mom's accident and how the thought of losing her made me realize she was my best friend. She wanted only the best for me.

"Please," I begged my fellow students, "tell your mothers you love them. Don't wait until it's too late, like I almost did."

I looked back at Mom. She beamed back at me, dabbing her eyes with a tissue.

"Mom," I said, voice quivering, "I ask you to forgive me. I ask *God* to forgive me."

As if on cue, one of Mom's Bible verses popped into my head.

"If we confess our sins, he is faithful and just to forgive us our sins."

*Thank you, God, for believing in me even when I disappoint you, just as I often disappoint Mom.*

Leaving the platform, I suddenly became aware of a new-for-me feeling, one that said, "It's okay, Shelly, to let your mom into your life. She won't always be here to guide you."

Instinctively, I reached up and caressed the silver pendant at my neck. My fingers traced the intricate lettering: Sweet Sixteen.

*Sixteen? Yes. Sweet? Hardly! But I will try, Mom*, I smiled through my tears. *I will try.*

# It's Not Fair!

### by Helen Grace Lescheid as told by Cathy Lescheid
ABBOTSFORD, B.C., CANADA

Visiting my dad in the provincial mental hospital had always filled me with dread. But on that drizzly day in December, as I mounted the massive stairway to the front entrance, I was excited. I had important news for my dad: in less than a week I'd be leaving for Switzerland to study at a Discipleship Training School. He'd be so proud of me when he found out that I earned the money myself and made all my own travel plans.

As Mom and I entered the smoke-filled lounge, we saw Dad sitting stiffly in a worn armchair beside a scruffy-looking Christmas tree. A television blared in a corner. Patients shuffled about the room or sat on the floor.

"Hi, Dad!" I said as cheerily as I could.

He turned his head in my direction. No smile, no glint of "I'm-glad-you've-come," only pain showed in his gray eyes. He motioned for us to sit down.

"Dad, I'm leaving home for seven months," I began.

No comment. *Hasn't he heard me?* "Dad, you know the Youth With A Mission school in Lausanne? Well, I'm going to study there."

He fastened his gray eyes on me. Not a spark of interest. Not a single question. Instead, Dad picked up a worn magazine and began to turn the pages.

Disappointment flooded me. Then rage. Dad might as well have slapped me hard across my face.

Driving home in the car, I yelled to my mom, "Why does he have to be so mean? Why can't he show a bit of interest in me at least once?"

Mom tried to tell me Dad's severe depression had frozen his emotions, but I couldn't accept her excuses for his behavior.

A few days later, when I boarded the KLM jet, I felt a bit scared. But mostly I felt relief. Visiting Dad in that dreadful hospital would not be part of my life anymore. I could now forget the pain of his rejections and get on with my life.

When I arrived at the Discipleship Training School, I couldn't believe the way people welcomed me. Their eyes filled with interest when I answered their questions about myself. Their voices were full of caring.

I enjoyed my classes. I was getting along great with my new friends. Every day held a special adventure, and yet there was one part of the day that upset me—the small prayer groups held after lunch.

An older staff person would encourage us to share specific needs in our lives. I knew I ought to say something about my dad, but I couldn't.

It came as a total shock one day when our leader prayed, "God, release Cathy from the hurt in her life. Help her to forgive the person who's hurt her."

I began to shake. My head felt stuffed. I fumbled around for a tissue. Quietly our leader handed me one and gave my hand a squeeze.

Later I told her about my dad. "He used to be at every single basketball game my brother and sister played in," I choked out. "He cheered so loudly that my mom tried to shush him up. But he's not been to even one of my soccer games."

"How long has your dad been depressed like this?"

"Four years."

"Cathy, you feel cheated out of an earthly father's love, don't you?" the woman said kindly. "But God wants to fill that void in your life. God is our Father—your Daddy! You are His very special girl, Cathy."

Well, I tried to picture God like that, but it was hard. A barrier loomed between me and God, so I couldn't get close to Him. *What is it, God? I want to know you as my very own Father. I want to hear you say I'm your very own special girl. Why can't I believe it?*

One day in class, I got a hint of what might be keeping me from a closer relationship with God. One of our teachers was speaking about bitterness. "When people hurt us we put up walls," he said. "We think this will protect us from more hurt, but often the worst enemy is inside those walls. That enemy is bitterness. It is one of the sins that nailed Jesus to the cross. Unless we get rid of bitterness, it will poison us and all our relationships—including our relationship with God."

That afternoon I stayed behind after our small-group prayer meeting to talk to our leader. "I know there's bitterness in my heart toward my dad," I said, "but what do I do about it?"

"Confess it to God and ask Him to forgive you," she smiled. "Then ask your dad to forgive you."

"Ask my dad to forgive me? Shouldn't it be the other way around? I mean, he's the one who hurt me!" I blurted out.

"Your dad's been hurt by your bitterness, Cathy," the woman said kindly. "You need to ask him to forgive you for that."

My cheeks were hot as I ran to my room. Grabbing my writing pad and pen, I hoisted myself to the top bunk. *Dear Dad,* I began. Then my mind froze. The words wouldn't come. *It's not fair!* Hot anger welled up inside. *Dad should be the one apologizing to me.*

I jumped off the bunk and began to pace.

"What's up, Cathy?" my roommate asked.

"Nothing!" I yelled as I fled out the door and down the steps. I'd go into the woods and work out. That always helped when I was upset.

An hour later I knew what I would do: I'd wait for my dad to write me first. He would ask me to forgive him. Then I'd say, "Oh, sure, Dad, I forgive you. Do you forgive me?" He'd say, "What for?" And I'd say, "Bitterness, Dad." Then he'd forgive me and we'd be friends again.

It only made sense that it should happen this way.

But it didn't. Instead, as the days went by, my uneasiness grew. I kept hearing our teacher's words: "Bitterness is like a sliver. If left alone, it will fester and get worse and worse. It will poison you and all your relationships. You must release the hurt to Jesus. You must let Him pull out the sliver. Confess your sin of bitterness to God and to the person who's hurt you. Only then can God heal you of the hurt."

Finally I couldn't stand it any longer. I knew if I didn't take care of the bitterness soon, I'd end up becoming a bitter person—like the ones I'd seen in the mental hospital. If I continued hurting Jesus with my bitterness, God would never become real to me.

I grabbed my blue-checked stationery and started to write.

*Dear Dad,* I began. *I want to ask you to forgive me.* Then the words just tumbled out. *I've had resentment in my heart toward you and I know I've hurt you. Dad, I love you. I have such sweet memories of you. I remember the times you helped me with my homework. You were so gentle and patient as I made the same mistakes again and again. I also remember the times we went canoeing and you kept encouraging me to go on, or told me to rest when I needed to. You are such a loving father and so patient. But I haven't been patient with you. Please forgive me. Dad, I love you so much.*

*Cathy*

I had finished my letter. Then I thought of something else to say. I grabbed a piece of white scrap paper and scribbled: *Dad, I haven't given up hope that you will be healed one day. The grace and mercy of God will heal you. Look up Psalm 147 verse 3. It's for you, Dad.*

Something happened to me while I was writing the letter. It was like pulling the plug on a sink full of dirty water. Something unclean and ugly left me, and all I could think about was how much I loved my dad and how much I didn't want to hurt him anymore. At the same time, the barrier between God and me had melted away. God's love for me felt so intense, it seemed He'd picked me up, twirled me about, and said in a laughing voice, "My most precious little girl. How I do love you!"

I had no idea how my dad would react to my letter. Would he even read it? Would he respond?

Exactly one month after I had written my letter, I pulled a blue airmail envelope out of the letter box in the office. A letter from my dad! The scrawled address told me Dad's hands had shaken badly.

Now, as I fumbled with the letter, I felt my heart race.

I plopped myself into the nearest chair and flipped the envelope over. Right over the seam of the flap Dad had written in his scrawled handwriting, *I Love you! God loves you.* Eagerly I ripped the letter open.

*Dear Cathy,*

*Thank you very much for your letter. It was so encouraging! God loves me and forgives me! I forgive you, dear, for everything. Please forgive me for being so callous, especially during your visits. I'm truly sorry. I love you very much and have happy memories of being with you. I am trusting God to make me well and take me home in due time. For a long time I did not pray or read the Bible. But God has forgiven me.*

*Thank you for sending me the Swiss chocolate bar. I enjoyed it! I miss you, Cathy, and love you very much. I hope you can read this letter. The lithium medicine makes my hands shaky.*

*Love, your dad*

I bounded up the stairs two at a time to my room. "A letter from my dad!" I shouted to my roommates.

I read and reread that letter. Not only had my dad said those powerful words, "I forgive you," but he'd asked me to forgive him. And his positive attitude surprised me. Was there a change in him?

When I had decided to make a U-turn and let go of my bitterness toward my dad, I'd done it mostly for my own healing; now it seemed healing was also coming to my dad. With God's love once more flowing between me and my dad, who could tell what wonderful things would happen next?

# Turning Point

by Amber Renee Medrano
PHOENIX, ARIZONA

I had never been in so much trouble. I looked up at the sky to fight back the tears stinging the corners of my eyes. My gut was in such a knot I wanted to vomit. Why did I do it? Why did I ever let her talk me into it? What was I going to do now?

There would be restitution, I was sure. I just couldn't believe I had let my best friend talk me into stealing money from purses in the girls' locker room. And now that everyone suspected me, I was going to have a bunch of upperclassmen coming after me, each to get their pound of flesh. Then there were my parents. My dad was going to *kill* me. I cried softly, nearly gagging on the lump in my throat. "God, please don't let him kill me."

Time stood still while I agonized over my fate. Mr. Norman was sure to notice my absence from the classroom. Urgency nibbled at my conscience to return to class. I took in a deep breath and forced my footsteps toward the lane that separated *Northwest Christian Academy* from *Sweetwater Church*. As I walked, I thought about who else knew of my crime.

As the following week went by, the high school gossip hive buzzed. During the scandalous swarm, I received many threats from fellow classmates. I was even cornered by a few varsity volleyball players. Luckily, I wasn't pounded into junior high hamburger, and somehow I survived the entire week. Friday afternoon came and I was a bundle of nerves. As I waited out front for my mother to pick me up from school, I anxiously wished the other shoe would drop. I was tired of being afraid. I contemplated telling my mother. In my mind, I pictured her calm and empathetic. This vision almost sold me on the idea to tell. As I watched our car pull into the parking lot, my stomach dropped again. I quickly resolved I would not tell her. I would figure out what to do on my own.

As I got into the car, she asked me how I was doing. This question caught me completely off guard. I tried to answer nonchalantly, but it didn't work. She pressed me for another answer, one that fit what her intuition whispered and my conscience conveyed. She told me that morning God reminded her of each time she had stolen money from her mother's purse. She said she couldn't figure out why. She asked me if I had something I wanted to tell her.

Instantly, conviction grabbed me with both hands. My stomach felt like the bottom simply dropped out altogether. The noise in my head was deafening, as every fiber of my being shouted "no" and "yes" at the same time. After a breathless pause, my lips quivered uncontrollably and the words just spilled out of me. I told her everything. I expected her to yell at me or even threaten me with "wait until your father hears about this!" Neither happened. Somehow she expected the news. Part of me thought, "Great, now I've got God telling on me," but mostly I was grateful and relieved.

When we got home, she told my dad. The anticipation of waiting for them to emerge from their bedroom was agonizing. As the cold sweat beaded on my forehead, I braced myself for his reaction. But the blowup never came. All during dinner, I couldn't look either of them in the face. I just cried. I knew I had let them down.

While dad thought about my punishment all weekend, I waited. Finally, after his evening prayer time on Sunday, he informed me of my fate. I was to write apology letters and hand-deliver each of them, along with the amount of money I had stolen. Since he was funding the money to pay everyone back, I would be in debt to him and therefore be working off the bill by completing special chores around the house, in addition to being grounded indefinitely. As Monday morning came, I was kept home from school to pen my apology letters. Putting it on paper proved to be difficult to do. After all, my terrible deed just stared back at me in black and white. I imagined what it would be like to confront my victims face-to-face the next day. I shuddered, and prayed hard I would be struck by lightning as I slept so I wouldn't have to go to school in the morning.

Out of all my victims, the reactions of four seniors sobered me the most. One of them was named Cheryl. She smoked and swore a lot, but she was very forgiving and didn't want to make a big deal of things with me. I knew she felt sorry for me, like maybe she had been in my shoes once before.

Erika was a tall, vivacious person and very competitive on the volleyball court. When I approached her with the envelope containing the letter and her money, she had a stern look on her face. As I came closer, she began to cry. She didn't make any sounds, but the tears came out from under her glasses and rolled down her cheeks. I couldn't tell if she was mad at me or just upset. I hoped she wouldn't slug me even though I deserved it. As I handed her the envelope, I looked at the ground. I tried to speak but nothing would come out. I slowly brought my gaze to meet hers and she abruptly looked away. Then, before I could attempt another word, she grabbed me and squeezed. I ended up with a mouthful of her jacket, but the embrace helped to heal both of our hearts. I knew I would not forget her intense compassion, or Cheryl's gift of dignity, and I hoped that someday I could be big enough to pass them on.

Robin was sort of weird, but she was also a wonderful girl that got along with everyone. Since she had become my mentor on the volleyball court, we were also good friends. She had desperately wanted to believe my lies throughout the ordeal, but when I approached her with the envelope, she was visibly stricken. All she could do was ask me, "Why did you lie?" I could only apologize again. I hated what I had done. I wished I could take it back and repair the friendship we once had, but I could not.

Alyna was a gruff, honky-tonk cowgirl. She was tough and loud and a real class clown. When I came to her with the envelope, she snapped it from my hand and gave me a firm lecture. I held my composure and waited until she was done, but inside I was shaking like a leaf. Then she hugged me. I couldn't believe it. She hugged me! Even so, after that encounter, I stayed out of her way for the rest of the year.

With all of that behind me, there was still the matter of the long walk to the principal's office. I knew Mr. Otto was a fair man, but I also knew what I deserved. I was lucky I hadn't been beaten up by half the high school already. And I was well aware that if I had been in public school, I would have gone home a lumpy, bloody mass. Plus, the administration would have involved the police right from the start. However, I knew Mr. Otto had chosen to handle this himself.

When I arrived, he suggested that I "take a seat." He began his next statements with a serious look. "Well, I want you to know I talked with your parents. I understand they've dealt with you in a fairly strict manner. Now, given your previous history, or lack thereof, since we both know you haven't had to visit me like this much, I am willing to go a little easier on you. Although, not by much."

After relaying my punishment, he continued to give me a pep talk. He reaffirmed his faith in me and praised me as a talented, bright young woman. I absorbed every word. I left his office in a strange bewildered fog, not sure of what had happened. It was too good to be true. I had been pardoned. Forgiven. My heart pounded in my ears. The air was so crisp and clean. My feet didn't touch the ground the rest of the afternoon.

That day I understood how complete redemption felt. Looking back, I'm thankful God loved me too much to let me get away with it. Through His conviction and mercy, I confessed. With one choice, I made it a turning point to start high school with a clean slate, a stronger character, and a more mature spirit. The next year, I was elected class treasurer.

# When Missy Rejected God

by Genetta Adair

EADS, TENNESSEE

*I'll never get my driver's license.* The thought consumed me as the conversation on the bunk below rambled on.

"I'm getting my license the day after I get home," one of the voices said.

I had nothing to say. I always knew I would never drive, and it had never seemed very important. But now, at almost sixteen, this simple fact spoke volumes about how different I was from everyone else my age. I was born legally blind.

Instead of seeing distances, my vision fades away. And beyond a few feet, details and definition become distorted. I can easily miss steps or curbs, and have even mistaken cardboard cutouts at the mall for people.

When I was three years old I had corrective surgery and eye therapy. Visits to multiple doctors followed. One doctor almost gave up on testing my vision because my memory was so good. When he left the room, I would run up close to the eye chart and memorize it. As soon as he returned, I recited the entire chart from twenty feet away. But he figured me out and prescribed contacts, providing only marginal correction. It was all he could do.

In spite of my lack of sight, childhood was fairly normal for me. Determined not to be different, I took gymnastics for five years and qualified for the competitive level team. And when my church youth group went on a twenty-mile hike up a mountain, carrying backpacks weighing sixty pounds, I joined them. I could barely discern the steep path and fell often, but I wasn't going to let anything stop me from fitting in with my friends. And nothing did, until now.

When my dad asked me what I wanted for my birthday, how could I tell him I wanted to ignore my sixteenth birthday?

"Do you want a party, honey?"

"I think I'd rather go away," I answered rather abruptly.

"Your mom and I want this to be a special birthday," he said. "We can go anywhere you want. How about Colorado?"

I love the mountains, and they're big enough for me to see. "Sure, Dad."

But even surrounded by the beauty of Colorado I couldn't escape the sadness. Clouds of depression hung over me, and not even the funky little tourist shops made me feel better. My mom and dad gave me a phone and my own phone line as a gift to indicate my independence. But it was still one of the worst times of my life.

How could this happen to me? How could God let this happen? *Don't you love me, God?* My conversation was quiet on the outside, but inside I was screaming. *Why?* I felt God had abandoned me, and I returned home feeling tormented.

While opening my locker after school one day, I heard a clanging and clinking sound. I looked up to find several classmates twirling car keys on their fingers.

"Man," a guy near me said, "I hate driving my old car. I wish I had a Mustang convertible."

My face burned. I ducked my head, trying to hide from this conversation.

"Yeah," a girl said, "but I'd like a Camaro instead."

Feeling hot all over, I took a deep breath. I knew I would be glad to drive anything. My friends drove me all over town, but I wanted more. I wanted the impossible—I wanted to drive.

One day I overheard friends discussing their spur-of-the-moment get-together the night before. "What are you talking about?" I asked. "Why didn't you invite me?"

"Well, Missy," one of them said, "we would have, but we all just met there and someone would've had to go pick you up." Then she simply turned and walked away. Her words stabbed me like a knife.

That night I turned to my dog, Muffy, for comfort. "Why can't they accept me like you do, Muffy? You never treat me differently." Hot tears rolled down my cheeks and I prayed aloud, "I don't understand. I've been faithful to you, God, but you let me down." Muffy licked my face and curled up close to my side. "Well," I said, "if this is the way it's going to be, I don't want any part of you." I refused to acknowledge God anymore. I gave up on Him—rejected Him. For the first time, my impaired physical vision destroyed my spiritual vision.

Month by month I grew more depressed. Every day was a bad day, and I cried all the time. I withdrew from friends so they wouldn't know. A year went by.

One night, while watching television, a car commercial started my tears flowing. I was completely losing it, and I knew I had a problem. I was broken and defeated. I felt empty, left out, rejected, and alone. I knew I needed to talk to someone about the way I was feeling, so I started down the hall. Mom was reading in bed, so I walked into her room.

"Mom, can we talk?" I squeaked. My throat constricted and tears popped from the corners of my eyes. Balancing on the edge of her bed, I asked, "Why would God allow me to live this way?"

Choosing to Forgive

Mom spoke with a gentle voice, "Missy, you can spend the rest of your life asking why, but you'll probably never get an answer." She reached for my hand. "You will grow lonely, bitter, and miserable." I knew that had already happened. Her voice slowed. "But you can ask God to show you 'how.'"

"How?"

"How your situation can be used for good. If you trust Him, He will show you."

I returned to my room, wondering if I could really do it. Could I trust God? Could I choose to ask "how" instead of "why"? I flipped on some music. Contemporary Christian tunes flowed from the speakers into my heart.

"Do you really know me well, Lord? Deeper than I know myself?" The words of this song helped me see that God understood when I thought that no one could possibly understand what I was going through. "I may never understand why, Lord, and I still don't think it's fair, but I need you back in my life." At that moment, I chose to embrace God again.

He took my weakness, combined it with my love of music, and created something to bring Him glory. By choosing God and His plan for my life, I sing and share my U-turn story to encourage others who feel empty, left out, rejected, or alone.

# God Forgives

by Helen Grace Lescheid as told by Susan Houle
ABBOTSFORD, B.C., CANADA

Throughout my high school years, my one true goal was to do extended mission service overseas, so when I received a letter from Youth With A Mission (YWAM), I was psyched. I worked for a year after high school graduation to save the money I needed to go.

Several weeks before I was to leave, the unthinkable happened. I found out I was pregnant. Me, Susan, the good Christian girl, who generally kept herself out of trouble—until now. I had just recently broken up with my boyfriend because I felt what we were doing was wrong, and asked God to forgive me. More than anything, I wanted to serve Him with my life. But now my life was ruined. YWAM would never let a pregnant girl participate.

I spoke to a spiritual counselor, Ida, at church, and I knew my next step was to inform my parents. My mom and dad were both incredibly accepting and supportive. All my life they had taught me when you do wrong, you admit it and take responsibility. Then you can receive God's forgiveness and healing. They urged me to talk to the pastor and elders at our church. They also forgave me and urged the congregation to accept me. And they did. But the most surprising news came with a phone call from Hawaii. YWAM still wanted me to come and serve with them!

That spring I flew to Hawaii to begin my seven-month service. Although the staff and my co-workers tried hard to make me feel accepted, I felt very different. As the weeks passed and my pregnancy showed more and more, I felt embarrassed to be a part of the

Choosing to Forgive

team. *They're just being nice because they're supposed to be.* Deep inside, I wished I'd never come.

The girls in the Mission gave me a baby shower, and in each small gift I found a Bible verse assuring me of God's love. *God only loves me because He has to. After all, He loves the whole world. But how could He possibly even like me now?* I struggled with the outpouring of God's forgiveness and acceptance.

Alone in my room that night, I knelt in prayer. "God, coming to Hawaii was a crazy idea. I can't share my faith with anyone. Who would listen to me anyway? They'll all take one look at my swollen stomach and say, 'Who do you think you are, talking about God?'"

*Susan, I do like you.*

Where did that voice come from? Was I imagining something, or was God really speaking to me? I held my breath and listened.

The quiet voice continued. *I'll show you tomorrow.*

The next morning, during my quiet time, I had a strong feeling that God had someone in particular for me to talk to that day. Later, while taking a walk along the beach, I noticed a man, about forty-five, sitting on a bench reading a newspaper.

*That's the one.*

I sat down on the far side of the bench and made several attempts to reach the man. "Sir, can we talk?" I repeated several times. The man never budged. My heart started pounding, my face flushed, and my palms became sweaty as old doubts washed over me. Who did I think I was, presuming to hear the voice of God? Of course this man wouldn't want to listen to me.

I got up and started walking away when I heard the quiet voice again. *This is the man I want you to speak with.*

"Okay, Lord, I'll try again," I whispered. "Excuse me, sir? God told me I am supposed to talk with you," I blurted out.

He dropped his newspaper and glared at me. His steel gray eyes scanned my flushing face, flitted across the bulge of my loose dress, and rested on my left hand. His annoyance was obvious.

"Who do you think you are?" he scoffed. "God told you to talk to me?" He cleared his throat. "I bet you're not even married."

"You're right, I'm not married." I spoke the truth. "I know what I did was wrong, but God has forgiven me."

The man stared at me, his mouth drawn into a tight line. Then his lips began quivering and his eyes became moist. The man was crying, his big shoulders heaving with each sob. He pulled a checkered hanky from his pocket and blew his nose. In a husky voice he said, "I have a daughter about your age. She serves God, just like you—sings with the Continental Singers."

"You must be very proud of her."

His eyes filled with pain. "My daughter got pregnant in high school." He turned away from me. "And I made her get an abortion."

"I'm sure she's forgiven you," I told him. I watched him stiffen and wring his hands together.

"I haven't been to church since."

"God forgives you." I moved just a little closer to him on the bench.

"But I can't forgive myself." His face twisted like he was going to cry.

"You don't have to feel guilty forever," I told the man.

He jumped up, his newspaper falling onto the sand. He turned and walked briskly toward the hotel. I jumped up and ran after him.

"Sir, God has forgiven you, please believe that," I yelled.

In the days and weeks to come, the reality of God's complete forgiveness worked its way into my heart. He told me what to say to the man on the beach, but He was also saying something to me between the lines: "Though your sins are like scarlet, they shall be as white as snow" (Isaiah 1:18). I recognized it immediately.

When my daughter was born, I named her Thalea, a Greek name for a flower just beginning to blossom. For ten years I raised her as a single mother, but God didn't intend for us to remain single. When I glided down the aisle of the church in my long white gown as my friends and family looked on, I knew it was not a day to dwell on my failures, but a day to celebrate God's grace in my life. I was as clean and pure as any bride, not because I had never sinned, but because Jesus Christ had washed me and made me "white as snow."

# choosing love

*If I speak in the tongues of men and of angels, but have not love, I am only a resounding gong or a clanging cymbal.* —1 Corinthians 13:1

A little love goes a long way. It makes people reach out to those who have hurt them, pray for those who don't want it, and forgive when logic says not to. In fact, there's nothing logical about love—on the surface, that is. But love is more than a concept or a warm fuzzy feeling in the pit of your gut. Love is choosing to do what is best for someone who can't find his or her way, choosing to love the unlovable, choosing to say, "I will believe the best in you when you forget to do that for yourself." It's choosing to do the hard thing because it is the right thing. Love is not just doing what Jesus would do, but letting Jesus do through you what needs to be done. Will you choose to love that extravagantly? Jesus did, for you.

# A Genuine Soldier

by Gail Dickert

HILLIARD, OHIO

I was not sure about the clothes she wore, the metal jewelry that pierced her tongue, or the rap song she wanted me to play for the congregation. I was sure, however, that she was a street soldier who was at war with the world. But this day, tears replaced a rough inner-city glaze that normally protected her face. I met Kay the day of her grandmother's funeral.

Alcoholism, hate, and generations of drug abuse and prison time tore Kay's family apart. Kay had not attended a youth group activity since she was twelve. Now, as a sixteen-year-old with a pierced tongue and heart, she returned to church to say good-bye to the only woman who had ever shown her God's love. Her grandma was gone, but in God's great plan, someone else was waiting for her, someone who was ready to love her—pierced body parts, bad language, attitude, and all.

The church hired me as youth director only a month earlier. I had a heart that beat for inner-city kids, and though I was not sure what the sound of that beat would be like, I knew I would march, eat, sleep, and drink its rhythm. I was standing in the back of this small inner-city church, wondering why God led me to serve in such a forgotten place. I wondered why I felt so led to come to the old woman's funeral. I had not met the young girl the pastor described as one of the youth group's "lost sheep." But once I heard about her, I could not stop myself from intruding on her grandmother's funeral.

Kay had always faced loss. As an inner-city kid, she experienced daily the loss of friends, family, and trust. It wasn't that everyone in her life had died; it was that everyone in her life lived as if they were already dead. Family relations were strained. Kay learned early the lie that "alcohol would make the pain of loss easier to deal with." One memory she hadn't allowed the alcohol to dull was what her grandmother said about God's love and His great plan for Kay's life. She wanted her grandmother's words to be true. She later told me she wasn't always certain what her grandmother's words meant, but the softness of her tone always remained a clear memory. Losing her grandma was like losing the only angelic voice Kay had ever heard.

At the funeral, I hugged Kay and offered to be her friend. I knew she needed someone to help her, but I was not sure if I was the right person. After all, I was only a month old when it came to inner-city work. However, the more I prayed for Kay, the more I realized I wasn't going to have to do anything. All I had to do was walk with Kay in her world. God was taking her somewhere, whether she knew it or not! I had the privilege of traveling alongside her on this journey of self-discovery that ultimately led this precious little street warrior into the United States Navy.

I remember her late-night phone calls steeped with deep questions about God and salvation. I remember how, as she fought the beauty of unconditional love, she yelled at me, "Why don't you just stop loving me already!" I remember how weekend after weekend she would apologize, hung over from partying all night.

I do not know why God took Kay's grandma away when He did. It was amazing how God reached past the pain of that death to bring life and joy. Inner-city life had hardened Kay. The death of her grandmother was just another reason for Kay to hate God and the world. I could not replace her grandmother, but God was there to give Kay what she needed, when she needed it. It was a blessing to play a part in the U-turn God orchestrated for her life.

# First Love

by Sandra J. Campbell
GARDEN CITY, MICHIGAN

It was definitely love at first sight. He had dark brown hair, root-beer brown eyes, and a smile that lit up his face and drew me to him. I would never forget the summer we spent learning lessons about love.

I was fourteen and had just finished junior high school. I was a pudgy girl with mousy-brown hair and thick, bottle-cap-lens glasses. Suffering from low self-esteem, I was desperately trying to find my niche in the world, but felt most comfortable alone. Awkward, self-conscious, and painfully shy, I had somehow found the courage to volunteer for the position of teacher's aid with the Head Start program at a neighboring elementary school. It was a program the federal government had started to help low-income preschoolers get a head start on entering kindergarten. That's where I met Arthur.

Arthur was only four years old. He asked to be in my group, and love was born. I learned through Arthur that to be wanted is a wonderful thing. Each morning I would wait for the big yellow school bus to pick me up. It was full of kids and other volunteers who needed transportation to the school. As it would pull up, I'd see Arthur's little face peering out the window, searching for me. He'd grin from ear to ear as I got on board. He always saved a seat for me so we could ride together. How thrilling it was for me to know that I was the reason behind his smile.

Most of the students in the program were from low-income families, so Head Start made sure they had a nourishing breakfast to begin their day. Arthur would only let me open his milk carton.

Choosing Love

Then we'd sit and talk about his day while he slowly ate each bite. It was nice to feel needed. As I helped him with many learning activities throughout the day I reveled in his successes. "Attaboy, Arthur!" spurred him on to excel in many areas. I learned that my praise could encourage him in all his endeavors. His sweet desire to please me was evident in every attempt. How precious it is to be valued so highly.

My "work" was never a chore, but a passion of my heart. Arthur taught me so much about love. I learned the reason you love someone is not just because of who they are, but also because of how they make you feel when you are with them. His doting attention made me feel beautiful from the inside out. He taught me I was of infinite worth. I began to see myself through his eyes, instead of through my own hypercritical inward gaze. It is a grand thing to feel so cherished.

The last day of summer school came much too fast. It was a sad day as I realized Arthur and I would probably never see each other again. I cannot explain the emptiness in my heart when the big yellow bus dropped me off at home. Arthur's nose was pressed hard against the window as he sadly waved good-bye. I turned and walked toward my house knowing I would never be the same. Arthur taught me how to recognize true love and rejoice in finding it.

Just a few months later I met my Forever Love when I was introduced to Jesus Christ. My best friend in junior high school invited me to come to church with her family. I began attending regularly with them and learned about God's love and His offer of a gift called eternal life.

One night at home my heart was troubled and I could not sleep. I realized that I was a sinner. I knelt by my bed and prayed for the Lord to forgive my sin, and I asked Jesus to be my very own personal Savior. All the guilt and burden of sin was lifted from my heart as I accepted God's unconditional love. My life made the greatest U-turn ever and has never been the same. I began an incredible journey through life accompanied by my Forever Love. My whole self-worth was no longer based on another's opinion of me, but on how precious I was to the Lord. Jesus Christ proved His love for me when He died on the cross for my sins. "Greater love has no one than this, than to lay down one's life for his friends" (John 15:13 NKJV).

Arthur taught me simple life lessons about love as this world knows it, but Jesus continues to teach me about His loving-kindness and mercies that are new every morning. I will be forever grateful for His precious gift of eternal life, and Jesus remains to this day my Forever Love.

# Where There Is Hope

by Bonnie Scheid

LITTLETON, COLORADO

The telephone rang, interrupting lunch with my son.

"This is Mel Schreiber, Public Defender's Office. I understand you are acquainted with Jimmy Dodge?"

"Yes, I am."

"Did you know Jimmy is scheduled for a detention hearing tomorrow morning?"

"No." I had lost track of Jimmy recently. He used to enjoy the coffeehouse at the church with our teenagers, Jeanne and John, but I also knew he had been in trouble recently for truancy.

"Let me explain," Mel continued. "Jim has just come out of the hospital from an overdose of his father's tranquilizers. He was admitted to a juvenile shelter until permanent disposition can be made. Jimmy tells me you might possibly provide a home for him until we can locate a boarding school."

"Did you say an overdose?" My interest turned to real concern.

"I want you to understand, Jimmy is in trouble at home, fighting continuously with his two younger brothers. His parents pressed assault charges, testifying that Jim is incorrigible. These charges will send him to some form of correctional institution. The overdose was a definite attempt to put an end to his life as the only way out of what he believes is an impossible situation."

He went on to tell me that both of Jim's parents are alcoholics, and just two months ago, Jim had intervened as the father was beating his sister, Jenny.

"We held him in detention but later released him back to the home. Jimmy was prepared to keep himself under control in spite of his environment, but was unable to hold his end of the bargain. He's missed appointments with his probation officer, has not attended his group therapy sessions, nor has he checked in with the Community Action Program as the court requested."

"Mr. Schreiber, he doesn't own a car or even have his license. Without parents to drive him to his appointments, I don't know how he would be able to cooperate with those requests."

"I agree, but the first need Jimmy has is a home. Are you willing to take him in temporarily? Like I said before, Jim thought you might."

After speaking with my husband later, I called Mr. Schreiber back and told him yes. "Tell Jimmy he has a place to live, and we'll meet you at the courthouse at nine o'clock Monday morning."

Our pastor, "the Rev," as he is commonly called by the teens in our congregation, met us at the hearing for support. Jim appeared from a side room, thinner than I remembered ever seeing him. And he was trembling visibly. At his side was Mr. Schreiber. The detention hearing was mercifully short, but detailed the fights with Jim's brothers and the parents' threats.

"Mrs. Byler, I understand you have a sixteen-year-old son at home. Jim's parents have called their son incorrigible. Do you still want this boy in your home?" Judge Franklin's concern for my home was evident.

"Your Honor." I looked at Jim, who was still trembling. "I think Jim would like to live a better life, but he needs an environment that offers him that chance. I would hate to think anyone was incorrigible at sixteen. Yes, Jim is welcome in our home." I noticed Jim take a deep breath of relief.

"In that case, I release Jim Dodge to your care until a suitable place can be found for his further schooling. In the meantime, he must meet certain conditions of his probation. One, he must visit his probation officer once a week. Two, he will attend group therapy at the county shelter. And lastly, he must apply at the Community Action Program in the next week to be admitted to a work/study program. And one more thing, Jimmy cannot visit his home unaccompanied or uninvited.

"Jimmy, do you agree to these conditions?"

"Yes sir, Your Honor." His voice was barely audible, but determination was evident on his face.

As Jim and I left the courtroom together, I grasped his arm proudly. We said good-bye to the Rev and thanked him for his support. As we passed Jimmy's mother, she told us she admired what I was trying to do, but she didn't think it would work. I watched Jimmy's eyes begin filling with tears, but just as quickly, his sadness was replaced with determination.

We headed for the nearest diner and I suggested a tall glass of milk and toasted sandwiches for both of us. Jim quickly downed the milk but ate only half of his sandwich.

"My throat is still sore from the stomach pump. I'm sorry. Can we save the rest?" Jim seemed concerned that I may consider him rude.

Next we stopped at the Community Action Program, learning that Jim would be trained for a job, working four hours a day, and studying three to four hours a day at the Adult Learning Center. He would earn a high school equivalency diploma, while at the same time earning pay for work hours.

Jim rode the bus faithfully to all of his appointments and therapy sessions, and he was proud of his job at the Social Security office where he dressed in a coat and tie. When he earned his first paycheck, he walked to the courthouse to find his public defense attorney, Mel Schreiber.

"Jim, you need to go right down that hall and knock on Judge Franklin's chambers. I'm so proud of all your hard work, and I know the judge will want to congratulate you, too."

In fact, Judge Franklin was so proud, he delayed his next case ten minutes so he could spend some time listening to Jim's good news.

As Christmas approached, Jim bought gifts for his family and wrapped a box of homemade cookies. "I want them to be proud of me."

Sometime later, a representative from the Children's Bureau came to the house to inform us that arrangements had been made for Jim's permanent placement. Everything was going so well, and Jim was within easy reach of his high school diploma.

"I've been accepted where?" Jim was shaking uncontrollably.

"You're supposed to check in at the Hilary House Drug Rehabilitation Center."

"But I've never been convicted on a drug charge. I'm not a drug addict."

I knew what he was saying was true. How could he be classified as a drug addict? By then he had been in our home for two months, and he was calm and content. If he were a drug addict, he would have been climbing the walls.

"I hear they shave your head when you go in there, and you have to earn back your hair." Jim told stories of the things he had heard about rehab centers, and I was equally concerned.

"Are you afraid of violence in there, Jim?" I asked.

"Anytime you have a bunch of druggies living together, there will be violence. These are guys who knock over little old ladies for their purses."

After speaking to Mel Schreiber, we set a new court date. We knew the stakes were higher now. We made it clear that we wanted Jim placed in our care rather than at the Hilary House. "Jim has kept all his appointments with you, and hasn't faced any other violations. We don't feel this is a good idea for him," I explained.

Fortunately, the new prosecuting attorney understood our reasoning as she interviewed us.

It wasn't Judge Franklin that day, but the appointed judge grasped the situation quickly, and Jim was given a suspended sentence on the overdose charge and released again into our care where he continued to be responsible to all his commitments.

Jim joined the Navy when he left us, still hoping to make his parents proud. He continued getting his life in order with Navy discipline and training. What began as a temporary assignment into our home taught him to take responsibility for his own life and actions. He learned that the world is full of hope and love. Suicide was not God's plan for his life. He also learned that God took his life full of pain and turned it around to a life of joy.

# If Only I Were Beautiful

by Amy Nicole Wallace

LAWRENCEVILLE, GEORGIA

I looked in the mirror and smiled.

He'd asked me out. An older guy from my church's singles group wanted to go out with me, a sixteen-year-old junior. He said I was beautiful.

I believed him.

So much so, that after we'd been dating a little while, his opinion dominated everything. Soon I dropped all my church activities because he didn't like them. He was my boyfriend and just wanted to spend time with me. It didn't matter that my mom and dad didn't like him. Or that my friends from church said things weren't right with our relationship.

I didn't care. I'd grown up an ugly duckling and finally felt like a swan. Someone wanted me. Someone who said I was the most beautiful girl in the world.

That same someone ripped away my virginity one night after hearing "no" too many times for his liking.

I didn't feel beautiful anymore. I felt like trash.

But I continued to go out with him. He never tried to force a physical relationship again. Instead, his anger escalated. He punched a wall out, barely missing my head. He damaged the nerves in my arm yanking me out of a car, accusing me of flirting with another guy.

Then he got in my face and yelled, "Don't even think about leaving me. No one else would want you anyway. You're used goods and I'm the best you'll ever get."

I believed him.

Until I moved away to attend a small Christian college in another city. There I met lots of guys who treated me with respect. But none of them ever asked me out.

Maybe my boyfriend was right. I was used goods, no longer beautiful.

I transferred in the middle of my freshman year to a state university in my hometown. My new friends encouraged me to get out and date other guys and not let my boyfriend push me around. So I did. I broke off our two-year relationship and jumped right into another one.

I moved in with my new boyfriend and spent the next few years trying to stay pretty enough to keep his attention. I played intramural basketball, weight trained, and played racquetball in my free time. On top of that, I held down a part-time job and managed to stay on the honor roll.

Anything to make me feel worthwhile, to feel beautiful.

It wasn't until seventeen years later as I sat in my family room surrounded by teens half my age, listening to them talk each week about boys and wishing they were beautiful, that I started to grasp the truth.

No one could make me feel beautiful.

One of the girls talked about her dad. "My dad says, 'You used to be so cute. What happened?'" Tears streamed down her beautiful chocolate skin. She didn't think she'd ever be beautiful.

I knew differently. She was already beautiful. She just didn't believe it.

Another night I posed a question. "What are you trying to get when you dress to impress a guy?"

Their eyes grew wide. I waited.

One of the older girls spoke up. "I like to dress nice. The boys notice and it feels good inside."

"But what happens when he decides someone else looks better?"

"It hurts."

"Yes, it does." I read the girls two quotes that God was using to change the focus of my search for attention:

"No love of the natural heart is safe unless the human heart has been satisfied by God first" (Oswald Chambers).

"We are not wrong to think we desperately need to be loved. We do. Our need does not constitute anyone else's call but God's" (Beth Moore).

I spent my teen years trying to get someone to love me any way I could. I wanted their attention and their words to make me feel beautiful. I took the questions of my heart to any guy who noticed. Do you see me? Am I beautiful?

Sooner or later everyone that answered "yes" fell under the weight of trying to make me feel okay.

What I've finally received in the deepest part of my heart is that our eternal need to be loved, to be beautiful, will be satisfied first in God.

Or it won't be satisfied at all.

So we're taking a U-turn together and encouraging each other to take our questions to God, not to boys, or anyone else for that matter. It's pretty amazing to see the light in the eyes of girls as they hear God answer their questions with, "Yes! I see you. You are beautiful. You are mine and you are loved."

I'm starting to see that light in my own eyes, too. I've stopped saying, "If only I could lose a few pounds. If only I were beautiful." Now I remind myself that I am beautiful in God's eyes. His eyes see me first thing in the morning and on bad hair days.

And He still says I'm beautiful.

Take a good look in your mirror. God has much to say. Listen closely. He is enthralled with your beauty.

# My Daddy's Lap

by Sharen Watson
HIGHLANDS RANCH, COLORADO

I remember clearly the night we left. I was eight years old and my brother was barely five. My parents had been divorced a year and my mother was taking my brother and me away from the only place we had ever called home, away from family and friends . . . away from our daddy.

I can still recall the sting of my tears and the dampness of my daddy's face as he held me close during those last few moments before we boarded the Greyhound.

"Daddy, I don't want to go! Don't make me!" I cried. "I want to stay here with you . . . please!"

"I know, Sharen . . . it's okay, honey," he said. "I'll miss you so much, but you need to go with your mom now. I love you . . . remember that."

Dad lifted me into his lap, trying to comfort me, but I desperately clung to his jacket, determined to never let go. I buried my head into his chest. His aftershave smelled like pine. It was a strong, familiar scent, and I breathed it in deeply so I wouldn't forget. His arms held me tenderly as we wept. I couldn't bear to look at his tears, but I knew. I felt his grief deeply.

So often before, my daddy's lap meant a place of comfort and rest, a place to quiet my childhood anxieties. Sometimes it was a place to hide when my brother confronted me with a squirt gun. But this was different, there was no comfort. . . . It was time to say good-bye.

In August, five years later, I went to visit my dad and found

Choosing Love

myself confronted with a competitor in the form of a new step-mother. She seemed to enjoy an occasional snuggle in my dad's lap as much as I did. I was thirteen years old.

Early one evening my dad and I sat in the family room watching television. I was on the floor enjoying my favorite summer treat, an orange Creamsicle. I raced the delicious drops of melting ice cream, trying to savor every bit of it before it reached my hands ... or worse, the front of my new overalls. Before licking the stick completely clean, I looked up and was horrified at the sight before my eyes. My stepmother had slyly made her way into *my* claim, *my* territory ... *my* daddy's lap!

Jealousy gripped my heart like a vise! With remnants of sticky ice cream all over my fingers and lips, I sprang from the floor and made a flying leap into what little bit of lap was left. There we were ... the three of us, tightly wedged into one regular-sized leather recliner.

Surprised, my dad looked at his wife, then at me.

"Well, isn't this cozy?" he said, not quite sure what to make of the situation.

I glared at my stepmother, looking resolutely into her eyes. The line had been drawn. It was either her or me. I was stubbornly determined to win the affection ... as well as the lap of my dad.

My stepmother, perceiving my resolve, quickly relented. She made up some poor excuse about getting supper ready, surrendering my dad's whole lap to me. I hugged my daddy's neck and struggled to find a comfortable position. I'm sure it wasn't easy for Dad, either, since I wasn't an eight-year-old child anymore. I was more than half-grown now, with the body and weight of a thirteen-year-old.

Pretending to settle in, I remained there for no more than a few minutes, trying to figure out a way to escape the awkwardness.

"I . . . I think I'll go help with dinner, Dad . . . okay?" I said as I carefully made my way out of his lap.

"Good idea, Sharen," he said, wincing in pain.

For a brief moment I thought I noticed relief spread over my father's face. I struggled to make sense of the whirl of emotions, made even more difficult by the presence of confusion and embarrassment, as I made my way slowly into the kitchen.

My stepmother, having a reasonably wise understanding of thirteen-year-old girls, turned and smiled knowingly at me. She held my gaze for just a moment. The wave of understanding that gently swept over me was a precious gift, paving the way for a stubborn, jealous young girl to take one of her first hesitant steps into womanhood.

"Would you like to learn to make fried chicken, Sharen?" she asked me.

"Can I?"

All of a sudden I felt just a little taller and a bit more confident, with an added dash of femininity, as my stepmother extended her hand, turning me toward the kitchen to awaiting chicken batter for the second lesson of my day.

# Bob's About-Face

by Laura Nixon

MOUNT VERNON, OHIO

Bob wasn't new to our church. For years his grandparents brought him. Yet for as long as any of us had known him, this withdrawn boy didn't talk. Because of his background, most people pitied him.

As a youngster, Bob's mom had abandoned him to his grandparents. For fourteen years they faithfully brought him every Sunday. Though he was regular in attending our youth group, he didn't say a word, participate in games, or even answer when we asked how he was doing. Week after week, Bob wandered into our teen room and slumped down on the sofa. Alone and with a vacant look on his face, his hollow eyes locked on the floor.

"Aw, he just needs to lighten up," many kids said. We all tried talking to Bob and urging him to join our activities, but he always held back. He'd silently shrug his shoulders and continue looking down.

Eventually most of us felt there was no way to reach him, so we stopped trying. Except for my friend Meg. She started sitting next to Bob each week. Even though he sat there silent, Meg would make comments and try to include him. She really worked on making him feel welcome. I watched, as everyone joined in organized games, Meg urged Bob to participate. When there were discussions, she asked for his ideas. Patiently and consistently, she tried to show Bob that he was accepted, that God's love wouldn't give up on him. Week after week my friend kept trying to be Bob's ally.

One Sunday, Mike, our youth pastor, announced, "We're going

on a camping trip next weekend!" We exploded with excitement. Everyone started chattering about packing and what to bring. Mike went on to explain that he wanted it to be a spiritual retreat as well as party time. "Oh, cool!" I shouted. "That sounds like fun," others said. A list circulated around the room and we all signed our name. Surprised, Mike noticed that Bob had signed up to go.

Friday night arrived. We all met at church with our sleeping bags, snacks, pillows, and overnight clothes. Everyone jabbered excitedly as the church vans loaded. Bob and his grandmother pulled up in their car and Meg and Mike ran over to greet him.

"Hey man, I'm glad you made it," I overheard Mike say as Bob climbed out of the car.

"Hurry and throw your stuff in the back of the van," added Meg.

Bob mumbled good-bye to his grandmother as he pulled his belongings out of the backseat. He walked with Meg and Mike to the van and tossed his things in with ours. Everyone was laughing and clawing their way to get a seat, but I noticed Bob quietly slipped into the front alongside Mike. As we pulled away from the church, our van was full of noise, music, talk, and laughter.

We finally arrived at the campsite and unpacked. After dinner, Mike shouted above the clamor, "Everybody around the bonfire!" The crackling fire welcomed us and soon we were all gathered in a circle. "Listen up," instructed Mike as he handed each of us a small white candle.

"I'm going to light my candle. Then I'll describe someone here tonight," he explained. "But," he continued, "I'm not going to tell you who it is."

"How will we know, then?" asked Ellie.

"When I'm done talking, I'll go over to that person and light his or her candle," Mike answered.

He explained that he wanted each of us to describe someone we admire and then light that person's candle. He said we'd continue around the circle until all candles were lit. With that, Mike began to describe someone in our youth group.

"There's a person here who is very faithful to church. He may not say much but he has a good heart," Mike said. He went on to share the good things he saw in this guy. Then, with his hand protecting the candle's flame, Mike walked over to Bob. He bent down and lit Bob's candle. Bob sat motionless; he just stared at the flickering flame. A hush fell over us and the only sounds were the occasional crack from the burning wood. It seemed like an eternity as we waited. Most of us had never heard Bob speak. I think Mike began to wonder if he'd made a mistake to light Bob's candle. Then Bob opened his mouth. Slowly he said, "There's somebody here who's always nice and talks to me." He said this person made him feel wanted more than anyone else ever had. Then Bob rose to his feet, walked past us all, and stopped where Meg was sitting. Her eyes filled with tears as Bob bent over and lit her candle.

Something happened that night. I believe God turned Bob around and touched every one of us on the trip. Soon Bob's look and expression changed. He was no longer a gloomy boy with hollow eyes who sat alone. Rather, he had confidence and began to open up and share with our group. Later, when we played games, Bob joined in. During devotions, his voice could be overheard talking to Meg.

"Sometimes we couldn't even get him to shut up," Mike joked later. Bob went on to make friends. We discovered he had a dry sense of humor but loved to joke around and act silly. Months later Bob mentioned to me, "When we were around that campfire, it was like a light had been turned on inside of me."

We are called to be disciples for Christ, to have His love light our world. God used my friend to be His worker. God made a U-turn in Bob's life . . . and in all our lives. It's what love is really all about, isn't it? Loving people who aren't always easy to love.

# Through God's Eyes

by Candace Carteen
BATTLEGROUND, WASHINGTON

By the time I was ten, I was totally ashamed of my father. All my friends called him names: Quasimodo, hunchback, monster, little Frankenstein, the crooked little man with the crooked little cane. At first it hurt when they called him those things, but soon I found myself agreeing with them. He was ugly. God and I knew it!

My father was born with something called Parastremmatic dwarfism. The disease made him stop growing when he was about thirteen and caused his body to twist and turn into grotesque shapes. It wasn't too bad when he was a kid; I saw pictures of him when he was about my age. He was a little short, but quite good-looking. Even when he met my mother and married her when he was nineteen, he still looked pretty normal. He was short and walked with a slight limp, but he was able to do just about anything. Mother said, "He even used to be a great dancer."

Soon after my birth, things started getting worse. Some other genetic disorder took over and his left foot started turning out to the left until it was almost backward. His head and neck shifted over to the right, his neck became rigid and he had to look over his left shoulder a bit. His right arm curled in and up and his index finger almost touched his elbow. His spine warped to look something like a big old roller coaster, and it caused his torso to lie sideways instead of straight up and down like a normal person. His walk became slow, awkward, and deliberate. He had to almost drag his left foot as he used his deformed right arm to balance his gait. I hated to be seen with him. Everyone stared. They seemed to pity me. I knew he must have done something really bad to have God hate him that much.

By the time I was seventeen, I was blaming all my problems on my father. I didn't have the right boyfriends because of him. I didn't drive the right car because of him. I wasn't pretty enough because of him. I didn't have the right jobs because of him. I wasn't happy because of him. Anything that was wrong with me or my life was because of him and the bad deed he had obviously done. If my father would have been good-looking like Jane's father or successful like Paul's father or worldly like Terry's father, I would be perfect! I knew that for sure.

The night of my senior prom came and Father had to place one more nail in my coffin—he had volunteered to be one of the chaperones at the dance. My heart just sank when he told me that. I stormed into my room, slammed the door, threw myself on the bed, and cried. "Three more weeks and I'll be out of here!" I screamed into my pillow. "Three more weeks and I will graduate and move away to college." I sat up and took a deep breath. "God, please make my father go away and leave me alone. He keeps sticking his big nose in everything I do. Just make him disappear so that I can have a good time at the dance."

I got dressed, my date picked me up, and we went to the prom. Father followed behind us in his car. When we arrived, Father seemed to vanish into the pink chiffon drapes that hung everywhere in the auditorium. I thanked God that He had heard my prayer. At least now I could have some fun.

Midway through the dance, Father came out from behind the drapes and decided to embarrass me again. He started dancing with my girl friends. One by one, he took their hand and led them to the dance floor. He then clumsily moved them in circles as the band played. Now *I* tried to vanish into the drapes.

After Jane had danced with him, she headed my way.

*Oh, no!* I thought, *She's going to tell me he stomped on her foot or something.*

"Candace." She smiled. "You have the greatest father."

My face fell. "What?"

She smiled at me and grabbed my shoulders. "Your father's just the best. He's funny, he's kind, and he always finds the time to be where you need him. I wish my father was more like that."

For one of the first times in my life, I couldn't talk. Her words confused me.

"What do you mean?"

Jane looked at me really strangely. "What do you mean, what do I mean? Your father's wonderful. I remember when we were kids and I'd sleep over at your house. He'd always come into your room, sit down in the chair between the twin beds, and read us a book. I'm not sure my father can even read," she sighed, and then smiled. "Thanks for sharing him."

Jane ran off to dance with her boyfriend.

I stood in silence.

A few minutes later Paul came up to stand beside me.

"He's sure having a lot of fun."

"Who?"

"Your father. He's having a ball."

"Yeah. I guess."

"You know, he's always been there. I remember when you and I were on the mixed-doubles soccer team. He tried out as the coach, but he couldn't run up and down the field, so they picked Jackie's father instead. That didn't stop your father, though. He showed up for every game and did whatever needed to be done. He was the team's biggest fan. I think he's the reason we won so many games. Without him, it just would have been Jackie's father running up and down the field yelling at us. Your father made it fun. I wish my father had been able to show up to at least one of our games. He was always too busy."

Paul's girlfriend came out of the bathroom and he went to her side.

My boyfriend came back with two glasses of punch and handed me one.

"What do you think of my father?" I asked out of the blue.

Terry looked shocked. "I like him. I always have."

"Then why did you call him names when we were kids?"

"I don't know. Because he was different and I was a dumb kid."

"When did you stop calling him names?"

Terry didn't even have to think about the answer. "The day he sat down with me outside by the pool and he held me while I cried about my mother and father's divorce. No one else would let me talk about it. I was hurting inside and he could feel it. He cried with me that day."

I looked at Terry and a tear rolled down my cheek as long-forgotten memories started cascading into my consciousness.

When I was three my puppy got killed by another dog, and my father was there to hold me and teach me what happens when the pets we love die. When I was five my father took me to my first day of school. I was scared. So was he. We cried and held each other that first day. The next day he became the teacher's helper. When I was eight I just couldn't do math. Father sat down with me night after night and we worked on math problems until math became easy for me. When I was ten my father bought me a brand-new bike. When it was stolen because I didn't lock it up like I was taught to do, my father gave me jobs to do around the house so that I could make enough money to purchase another one. When I was thirteen and my first love broke up with me, my father was there to yell at, to blame, and to cry with. When I was fifteen and I got to be in the honor society, my father was there to see me get the accolade. When I was seventeen, he put up with me no matter how nasty I became or how high my hormones raged.

As I looked at my father dancing gaily with my friends, a big toothy grin on his face, I suddenly saw him differently. His handicaps weren't his; they were mine. I had spent a great deal of my life hating the man who loved me. I had hated the exterior that I saw and I had ignored the interior that contained his God-given heart. I felt very ashamed. I asked Terry to take me home.

On graduation day at my Christian high school, my name was called and I stood behind the podium, honored as the valedictorian of my class. As I looked out over the people in the audience, my gaze stopped on my father in the front row, sitting next to my mother. He sat there in his one and only suit holding my mother's hand and smiling.

"Today I stand here as an honored student. I have been able to graduate with a 4.0 average. I've had the ability to stay in the honor society for three years. I was elected class president for the last two years. I led our school to championship in the debate club. I even won a full scholarship to Ohio State University so that I can continue to study physics and someday become a college professor. What I'm here to tell you is that I didn't do it alone. God was there, and I had a whole bunch of friends, teachers, and counselors who helped along the way. Up until three weeks ago, I thought they were the only ones that I would be thanking this evening. If I had thanked just them, I would have been leaving out the most important person in my life: my father."

I looked down at my father, and the look of complete shock covered his face.

I stepped out from behind the podium and motioned for my father to join me on stage. He made his way slowly, awkwardly, and deliberately. He had to almost drag his left foot up the stairs as he used his deformed right arm to balance his gait. As he stood next to me at the podium, I took his small crippled hand in mine and held it tight.

"Sometimes we only see the silhouette of the people around us. For years, I was as shallow as the silhouettes I saw. For almost my entire life, I saw my father as someone to be made fun of, someone to blame and someone to be ashamed of. He wasn't 'perfect' like the fathers my friends had. What I found out three weeks ago is that while I was envying my friends' fathers, my friends were envying mine. That realization hit me hard and made me look at who I was and what I had become. I was brought up to pray to God and hold high principles for others and myself. What I've done most of my life is read between the lines of the Good Book so that I could justify my hatred."

I turned to look my father in the face.

"Father, I owe you a big apology. I based my love for you on what I saw and not what I felt. I forgot to look at the one part of you that meant the most, the big heart that God gave you. Father, as I move out of high school and into life, I want you to know that I could not have had a better father. You were always there for me, and no matter how badly I hurt you, you still showed up. Thank you!"

I took off my mortarboard and placed it on his head.

"You're the reason that I'm standing here today."

I felt God's light shining down upon me as I embraced my father more warmly than I ever had before. We both cried.

For the first time, I saw my father through God's eyes, and I felt honored to be seen with him.

# choosing to pray

*He has delivered us from such a deadly peril, and he will deliver us. On him we have set our hope that he will continue to deliver us, as you help us by your prayers. Then many will give thanks on our behalf for the gracious favor granted us in answer to the prayers of many.*

—2 Corinthians 1:10-11

Sometimes it seems like prayer is such a small thing that it can't do any good. And then there are days it feels like time wasted. But God has told us to bring our petitions and thank-yous to Him. He already knows our needs, even before we do. However, praying is a sign of trust, of going to the Source, of knowing Who is in charge. Prayer is that open communication that lets us know His heart as well as our own. When ancient Israel went to war, it was the priests and praisers who went first. Choose to lead with prayer and watch expectantly for God to move.

# Giving From the Heart

by Wendy Dunham
BROCKPORT, NEW YORK

Only four teens were left waiting for their ride home. While waiting, they helped straighten chairs, take down balloons and streamers, turn off the lights, and lock the church doors. It had been a special youth event—a surprise send-off party for their youth leader, Mark.

Mark was scheduled to leave the next day for a one-year overseas mission trip.

Without warning, thirteen-year-old Serena walked over to Mark. She reached in her pocket and pulled out a large roll of money.

"Here, Mark," she said, "I want you to have this for your mission trip."

Surprised, Mark replied, "Where did all that money come from?"

"I've been baby-sitting after school, and I've saved the money for you," Serena explained.

Overwhelmed by the depth of her generosity, Mark said he couldn't accept such a gift.

"Please," Serena continued, "I have prayed about it and I truly believe this is what God wants me to do with the money."

After talking to Serena's mother, Mark decided to accept her gift.

Many years passed before Mark and Serena saw each other again at their youth group reunion. They talked and shared with each other what had been happening in their lives. Serena was a sophomore in college, doing well, but barely making financial ends meet. Mark was also doing well—he had married and had two children. Before the reunion was over, Mark and Serena exchanged addresses.

Several weeks later Serena sat in her dorm room wondering how she would pay for her new semester's books. "Lord, I know you will provide for me. Please give me the faith to believe you will take care of my needs."

Suddenly her roommate burst into the room. "Mail call for you, Serena!"

Full of excitement, Serena grabbed the letter. As she tore open the envelope, a check fell to the floor. Here's what the letter said . . .

*Dear Serena,*

*It was such a pleasure talking with you at the reunion. I'm thrilled to know you continue to walk with our Lord, and that you are studying for the ministry. I believe the Lord has mighty plans for you.*

*I'll always remember you as a young teen, and how you gave of yourself so freely to support my mission trip. Your generosity and desire to do God's will blessed my life . . . now I want to do the same for you.*

*Love in Christ,*
*Mark*

God had answered her prayer for the much-needed book funds, providing for her as she had helped to provide for Mark so many years before.

# Close Encounter

by Linda Evans Shepherd
LONGMONT, COLORADO

"Be careful what you pray for" should have been the instruction I gave my kids when I was their summer youth director. If I had known how dangerous getting what you pray for can be, it would have been.

"Let's pray for a miracle," I told the group at the small southwest Texas church where I worked during my summer break from Lamar University. "Let's dream up a prayer that seems too big for even God, and let's see what He does with it."

Veronica, a tiny teenager with dark brown hair and eyes to match, raised her hand.

"You've been teaching us how to tell people about Jesus," she said. "Let's pray God will give us the chance to witness to our town's two gang leaders!"

I gulped, thinking of the two tough teens who smuggled drugs over the Mexican border for the local crime syndicate. "All right," I said, "why not? Let's pray we'll get a chance to witness to Mundo and Manuel."

We all bowed our heads and prayed earnestly. Despite our prayer for a miracle, I felt safe. The tough teens we were praying for were not likely to poke their heads around our church. I was not likely to see them on the street.

The summer went by fast, full of fun and excitement. We swam often in the Frio River. We worked hard on our prayer notebooks—a concept I had discussed with the youth group earlier and they were all excited about. Several of them went to a retreat at a local campground. The week of vacation Bible school, I was relieved and excited to have help from Rachel, a college girl my own age. It was an amazing and successful week, ending with parents' night, where we stood by proudly as our young charges sang and signed *Jesus Loves Me* in American sign language.

Afterward, the stars above the west Texas town twinkled in a cloudless sky as Rachel and I waited in the deserted parking lot for the pastor to drive us home. I noticed two teen boys walking down the road toward the church. The streetlight broke the shadows as they approached and revealed their faces. My heart pounded. It couldn't be. The faces belonged to Mundo and Manuel, the teen drug runners my youth group had been praying for.

I watched the boys advance and knew it could mean trouble. When they passed us by I drew a breath of relief. A few minutes later the boys returned for a second go-around. I tried to ignore them.

"Hey, Linda!" a drunken voice called out.

Goose bumps spread up my arms. Bad sign. *They've been drinking and they know my name, even though I've never met them!*

"What do you want?" I called into the darkness.

"Come over here!"

Rachel shouted back, "No, you come over here!"

The two young men approached. Even under the dimness of the streetlight, I could see hate filling their bloodshot eyes.

"What do you want?" I repeated, trying to sound calm.

Manuel stepped forward and crowded me with his alcoholic breath. I stepped back, trying to escape the fumes. "What do we want?" Manuel slurred. "We want you to prove that God is real!"

I swallowed hard. "God loves you. His Son died for the things you've done wrong. In fact, John 3:16 says, 'God so loved the world that he gave his one and only Son, that whoever believes in him shall not perish but have eternal life.' If you ask Him, He will forgive your sins and He will be a part of your life forever."

"I don't want you to tell me about God; I want you to prove to me that He is real," Manuel replied, stepping even closer.

"I can only prove it by telling you He is in my heart."

Manuel towered over me. His voice shook with anger, "That's not good enough. We want you to prove there is a God, and we want you to prove it NOW!"

As Manuel encroached into my space, I backed into a wall. Now I could back no farther. I glanced around nervously. There's nowhere to run and no one to help! *Lord*, I prayed silently, *there is nothing more I can say to these men to prove you are real. Would you please take over now? It's up to you.*

As I finished my quick prayer, the beautiful starry night changed. A strong wind rose up. Swirling dust pelted our faces. High above our heads, a cloud blotted out the stars and broke the blackness with jagged streaks of lightning. Everyone froze while the wind whipped our hair and blinded our eyes. Rachel shouted above the booms of thunder, "See, that is God telling you He is real!"

No one argued. The frightened boys ran one way and Rachel and I ran the other. A few minutes later, the cloud passed and calm returned. By the time the pastor had driven us back to my house, we were still awestruck. We sat on my bed in the safety of my little bedroom and smiled at each other.

"You know," I said, repeating myself for the one-hundredth time, "that really was God. He really was there."

"Yes," Rachel agreed, nodding as if in a trance. "He was awesome!"

The excitement of our discovery gave us a sleepless but joyful night. I learned God can reveal himself not only to two naïve college girls, but also to two drug runners who dared to ask for proof of His existence. I learned to be careful about what I choose to pray for, and I also learned to pray for whatever impossible dream He may put into my heart. After all, I'll never know which miracles God is willing to perform unless I dare to ask.

# A Handle on Our Prayers

by Carol Genengels

SEABECK, WASHINGTON

Mark and Bud were excited about their much-awaited adventure to a Christian retreat in Canada. They were saving the needed funds by working hard in the hot sun, chopping and splitting firewood.

Bud wiped sweat from his brow and heaved a mighty swing to his log. *Swack. Crack.* The sounds echoed as the ax struck the wood and the handle shattered in his hands.

Now what was he to do? His dad would be really upset about the broken handle. Hiding it behind the shed, he decided to tell his father after he and Mark came back from the retreat. By then he might have found a way to pay for a new handle.

The retreat was great. Bud and Mark swam, hiked, sang, ate, and attended devotions with kids from around the United States and Canada. They both came home refreshed and renewed in their commitment to make a U-turn back to the Lord and His wishes for their lives.

Seeing his dad standing with the broken ax handle quickly evaporated the newfound joy and peace.

"Just what do you plan to do about this?" he asked.

"Dad, I promise I'll find a way to replace it. Just give me a few days."

"I certainly hope so. You broke it and you need to find a way to get it fixed."

"I will, Dad, you'll see," he said.

When Mark's mom walked in on them a few days later, she

knew something was wrong. Both boys were deep in conversation with worried looks on their faces.

"What's up, guys?"

Mark told his mom Bud's entire story of the ax handle and how they needed a way to replace it, and soon.

"Bud's dad is expecting him to do something soon to get it fixed," Mark told her. "We have chosen to turn the entire problem over to the Lord. Can you help us pray and ask God to find us an answer?" he asked her.

Ann never took a prayer request lightly. She started praying right away for Bud and his dad.

The very next day she made a call to one of her friends.

"You might think I'm crazy," she said to her friend, "but I have been praying about something, and every time I do, I keep seeing your face and hearing God tell me to call you."

Her friend asked what it was all about. Ann explained about the broken ax handle and the trouble Bud would get into if he couldn't replace it.

Suddenly Ann heard laughter on the other end of the phone. Her friend couldn't seem to stop laughing.

"What's so funny?" Ann asked.

"This is just too much!" Her friend said, chuckling. "God certainly does work in mysterious ways. A man owed my husband money for a job he did and couldn't pay in cash. He paid us with a bundle of ax handles, all different sizes."

"Well I'll be!" Ann laughed.

"Tell Bud to come over and pick out any size he needs, free of charge."

The next day Bud proudly presented his father with a brand-new ax handle. He told his dad how God had answered his prayer and found it for him.

Bud's dad listened intently as he admired the fine new handle. He admitted he needed to learn more about a God who cared so much about a teenager's problem.

This started a U-turn in Bud and his father's relationship, as well as for Bud's dad's relationship with the Lord.

No matter what our age, no matter what our problem—even if it's needing a new ax handle—when we choose to bring our problems to God, He shows us He truly cares.

# Winning Is More Than a Score

by Jeanne Pallos as told by Dave Tepper

LAGUNA NIGUEL, CALIFORNIA

My problems started my freshman year, when my parents bought a new house and ripped me away from all my old neighborhood friends. As if that wasn't bad enough, they decided it was time to toss me into the sea of life, and they pulled me out of the small, sheltered Christian school I'd attended since second grade.

Don't get me wrong. I was sick of the rules and regulations in my Christian school. It was fine when I was a kid, but I was tired of being told how to wear my hair, what kind of clothes to wear, and how to talk.

I wanted freedom. For years I'd dreamed about attending public high school with my neighborhood friends and playing football. Now, at fourteen, I had the public school, but no friends and no football.

My Bible-thumping friends from the Christian school were replaced by kids with baggy clothes, pierced body parts, and dyed hair—the kinds of kids we used to pray for and stay away from. Now these losers—as some folks called them—were my best friends. They were the only kids who understood me and didn't make fun of me.

Most of all, these kids—like my new best friend, Jerry—were just like me—scared on the inside. Jerry said he felt like a loser, too.

When the school year started, I had lied to my mom and told her I was going out for freshman football. As if I was good enough to make the football team. I knew they'd laugh me off the field. So Jerry and I hung out at Taco Bell during practice, but I'd always be at the school curb waiting for my mom when practice ended.

My mom got suspicious when my football clothes showed up in the laundry week after week looking brand-new. No grass stains. No mud.

So what did she do? She called the football coach and the high school principal. "He's not on the team," they told her.

I was busted.

Two days later I sat at a round table in the principal's office, surrounded by all my teachers, my parents, the principal, and Coach Brown, the head football coach, who was also my phys ed teacher.

"Dave doesn't fit the profile of a failing student," the math teacher said.

"He's always quiet in class but doesn't do his assignments," my English teacher said.

Wringing my sweaty hands, I stared down at the table, thumping my leg up and down, and hiding under my baseball cap.

Coach Brown looked at me. "You know, Dave, I can't figure this out. You're one of the most talented kids I've ever had in PE. You're thoughtful of the other kids, and I never have to tell you to include anyone in a game. Most kids aren't like this. They only pick the best players, but not you. You seem to care about everyone."

*Who is this guy talking about?* I wondered.

"In fact, I'd love to have you on the football team, but . . ."

*Here it comes. I knew this couldn't last.*

"Grades and attending classes are far more important than playing football. No matter how much talent you have."

I blocked out the lecture. I'd always dreamed of playing football. In my own head, I was a great quarterback. All I had to do was close my eyes and I could see the crowd, hear the cheers, and feel the thrill of throwing the winning touchdown. If only I had had the courage to sign up for the team.

Just then the first-period bell rang. A quick good-bye to my parents, and I bolted.

Coach Brown invited me to his office to study. Sometimes, though, we'd just hang out and talk football.

I'm not sure what changed—maybe it was having Coach Brown for a friend—but suddenly more kids talked to me now. Even guys from the football team treated me like a normal kid.

Spring tryouts came. "Are you going to go out for the team?" my friend Jerry asked. "You should do it."

"Nah, not this year."

"Come on, man. You know this is what you want."

How do you tell your best friend that you're just too scared?

I'd sneak around practice and watch the coaches working with the kids. There was no way I could compete with those guys who'd been playing football since they could crawl.

"You know there's a spot for you on the team," Coach Brown said when he saw me hanging around the practice field. "It's up to you."

By spring tryouts of my junior year, I felt it was too late to join the team. I beat myself up, wishing I'd gone out the last two years. *Just too chicken,* I reminded myself. Now Coach would never let me on the team.

"Dude," Jerry said, "this is your last year to go out for football. You'd better do it."

"Nah," I said. "I can't compete with those guys."

Then he grabbed my arm. "Man, I'm walking you to that locker room, and I'm not leaving until you sign up for the team. I'm not letting you out of it this year."

That's how I ended up on the varsity football team the fall of my senior year.

Coach let me try out for quarterback. Every time they tossed me a snap, I dropped the ball. But the funny thing was—no one laughed.

Guys would high-five me in the locker room and tell me I was doing a good job. Me. The guy who couldn't catch a football.

One Saturday, Coach scheduled a junior varsity game with the toughest school in our league. Not only was I the only senior on the JV team, but I was the only quarterback. Jerry and my parents were there to watch me actually play in a game.

When we lined up for the scrimmage, something strange happened. "Please, God, help me catch this snap." I wasn't swearing. I was praying. Just like I used to do when I was a little kid in the Christian school.

The ball slipped through my nervous fingers like a greased watermelon. But every time I came out of the game, the varsity players, who came out to watch the game, patted my back, and Coach said I was doing a great job.

Even though we lost 30–0, no one put me down. Players high-fived me as we ran back into the locker room.

The season was almost over, and I knew I'd never play in a varsity game. Week after week, I suited up and stood on the sidelines.

Then it happened. Homecoming. Packed stadium. Marching bands. Bright lights. Fourth quarter and our team was winning by twenty-five points.

I wasn't thinking anything, but then I heard, "Dave, Dave, Dave . . ." coming from the players on the sidelines. They turned and started waving towels over their heads toward the stands. Kids and parents joined the chant: "Dave, Dave, Dave . . ."

With four minutes left in the game, Coach called me over. "Dave, I'm putting you in—as quarterback."

No time to be nervous. I put my helmet on and trotted onto the field as if I'd done this a thousand times.

I bent down for the snap and started to swear under my breath. But I stopped. "God," I prayed instead, "please help me not to blow it."

The ref's whistle blew, I caught the snap, then handed the ball off to the tailback. He ran down field and got tackled. We lined up again. "Please, God . . ."

The ball didn't slip through my fingers. I looked down field and threw. The ball landed on the ground.

Back to the line of scrimmage. I handed it off again, and we got a first down.

When the game clock ran out, the players were all over me.

A few weeks later, at the end of the Senior Awards Banquet, Coach walked to the mic and looked over the crowd of parents and players. "We've given out all our awards but one. I consider this the most important award of all. This is the only award chosen by the players, not the coaches."

He went on. "This award is for the player who shows great courage and wins the respect of all his teammates. Dave Tepper, please come forward. You have been voted Most Inspirational Player by your teammates."

In my heart, I knew God had answered my prayers. I couldn't wait to show Jerry my award and thank him for pushing me onto the team.

# choosing life

*The thief comes only to steal and kill and destroy; I have come that they may have life, and have it to the full.* —John 10:10

You've probably heard it somewhere (especially when we say we *have* to do something) that "life is a choice—the only thing we *have* to do is die." And although usually said flippantly, the words are still true. Everything we do, say, and embrace is a choice—including allowing someone else to choose for us. God has set life smack dab in front of us—a gift like no other. And before we can choose what to do with it, we have to choose to accept it. Let's choose life, throw our arms around our heavenly Father, and thank Him for the adventure. It won't always be easy, but it's a one-of-a-kind gift He's planned just for us. Choose life!

# Just Trust Me

by Heather Tomasello

RICHMOND, VIRGINIA

I locked the drugstore bathroom stall and took the box I'd just purchased out of its plastic bag. Two minutes later, I had the results I'd been dreading. Two pink lines. I struggled to choke back my tears as I read the description for the millionth time. *Two lines indicate a positive result. This test is 99 percent accurate.* There could be no doubt. I was pregnant.

*What am I going to do?* I wondered. *How am I going to tell my mom? Why me, God?* The last thought surprised me. I hadn't been on speaking terms with God for quite some time. A few months earlier, just after my sixteenth birthday, I decided to quit going to church.

"I just want to take time off," I told my youth pastor. I didn't share with her the questions keeping me tossing and turning at night. Do I believe in God just because I've been told to all my life? Or because I think He's real? How can I ever know for certain? Everyone at church talked about how important it is to let God be in charge of your life, but *I* wanted to be in control. So God and I were at an impasse. I told Him to leave me alone; I wanted to live life on my own terms.

Now, as I stared at the pregnancy test, I was angry with God. Why did He let this happen to me? I also felt guilty. How could I have been so stupid? I was in way over my head and I knew I needed help. But I was the one who told God to leave me alone. I couldn't turn to Him, not after this.

God Allows U-Turns for Teens              120

"What are we going to do?" I asked my boyfriend after giving him the news.

"We're not ready to be parents. We have our whole lives ahead of us! We both want to go to college," he said, shaking his head. He added softly, "I think you should have an abortion."

His words made my heart sink, but I decided he was right. If I had an abortion, no one would ever have to know about our mistake. It would all be over quickly and we could get on with our lives.

With a heavy heart, I made an appointment at an abortion clinic. But as the day drew closer, so did my doubts. Could I live with this decision? Would two wrongs make a right? A few nights before the appointment, I had a dream. I saw myself holding a baby—a little boy with curly brown hair. In my dream, I heard God speaking to me.

"Don't kill your son."

"But God," I protested. "I'm not ready to be a mother."

"I know," He replied. "I've already chosen a family for your baby. Just trust me."

I woke up shaken, but I knew what I had to do.

"Let's have the baby and put it up for adoption," I told my boyfriend.

"How are we going to do that?" he asked.

"I don't know," I said. "But God will help us."

For the first time in my life, I knew—truly knew—God was real, that He cared about me and I needed Him. I prayed simple, fumbling words.

"Dear God, please forgive me for turning away from you," I said. "Please help me do the right thing."

I chose life, but the next nine months were the most difficult in my life. My mother, boyfriend, and close friends were supportive, but many classmates were insensitive and cruel.

"Why didn't you just have an abortion?" some asked.

"How can you give your baby away?" others judgmentally said.

I often wondered the same things as I felt myself becoming attached to the kicking, squirming baby growing inside of me. "Lord, how will I be able to go through with this?" I asked.

"Just trust me," He answered.

My boyfriend and I spent hours at Social Services, looking at letters and pictures from families who wanted to adopt. I prayed over each file, but none seemed right. Finally, on one visit our social worker told us, "I spoke to a couple yesterday and told them about you. They said that they want to adopt your son. They asked me to pull their file from circulation so no one else can consider them. They want to talk to you as soon as possible."

That afternoon we telephoned Jack and Shelley. As I talked to them, I knew they were the family from my dream—the family God had chosen for my son. I met them face-to-face a few months later when I placed a beautiful baby boy with curly brown hair into their arms. They named him Brett.

"He's wonderful," Jack said as he cradled his new son. "Thank you so much!" Shelley hugged me. I was happy for them, but on the drive home, I couldn't stop sobbing. I knew what we had done was right—but it still hurt.

"What if they don't love him as much as I do?" I cried. Then I felt God's peace envelop my heart like a hug.

"Just trust me." He had enabled me to make the hardest decision of my life. He had turned my mistake into a blessing—for me, my little boy, and his new family. And, most importantly, even when I'd asked Him to leave me alone, He didn't.

How could I not trust Him?

# Jonny's Gift of Life

by Ann Jean Czerwinski
ERIE, PENNSYLVANIA

For fifteen years, Jonny shared the gifts God gave him with everyone he knew. He was outgoing and funny. He loved his family and was never afraid to show it. He treated his friends like they were part of his family. He was a role model to the younger kids in the neighborhood, and he loved teaching them about the things he enjoyed.

Bike riding was one of Jonny's passions. Flying is actually what you would have to call it. He loved the challenge of racing his bike over wooded paths and city streets. He lived to take his bicycle airborne at any given opportunity. Children in the neighborhood gathered around Jonny as he gladly showed them how to do the tricks he had mastered. It was his gift, and he loved sharing it.

On September 22, 2000, Jonny Billingsley was riding his bike with his buddies along the streets of his Erie, Pennsylvania, neighborhood. Without a care in the world, he defied gravity over the pavement, with wings of freedom that only his bike could offer.

But this was the last night Jonny would ride his beloved bicycle. He collided with a truck on a busy city intersection, and not even the best medical intervention could have saved him. The only consolation left for his family was the fact that he died doing what he loved most, riding his bike.

It was during this terrible tragedy that Jonny's mother, Michelle Billingsley, recalled a conversation she had with her son in April of that year. He told her he wanted to be an organ donor, and that as soon as he received his driver's license, he would make sure it would say *organ donor* right on it. His mom was surprised with how the conversation came about and relayed it in our interview.

"Jonny's sister, Katie, was sitting at the table talking to me about a school assignment for her high school ethics class. Their assignment was to write a living will. While we were talking about her being an organ donor, Jonny walked into the room. He listened for a while, and I could tell he was giving it deep thought. He finally said, 'I think it's a good idea. I'm a strong kid. If anything ever happened to me, I would want my organs to be donated.'

"I asked him if he knew exactly what that meant, and he answered with certainty, 'What if someone out there is having a problem with their heart or kidney? Why would I need to keep mine if I were dead? If someone else can use them, then that's what I want.' I just smiled and winked at him and told him I would keep that in mind."

Mrs. Billingsley went on to say, "So that's how it all came about. When we were thrust into that position, there was no decision to make. It was a request we had to honor."

And that's exactly what happened. The night of the accident, when Jonny was declared brain-dead, his parents met in the cool night air outside of the Hamot Medical Center. They looked at one another and knew exactly what Jonny would tell them to do. The words were difficult to find, but they called on their faith and prayed for the Lord's strength to make this decision.

Once Jonny's request was made known to the doctors and the representatives of the Center for Organ Recovery & Education, a series of tests were performed to determine brain death, a routine procedure for organ recovery.

Because of Jonny's decision, a thirty-six-year-old mother of four in Philadelphia received a healthy heart; a fifty-six-year-old man

Choosing Life

from West Virginia received a liver; a retired psychologist in Washington, D.C. is the recipient of the left kidney and pancreas; and ironically, a fifteen-year-old boy in Virginia received a new right kidney. Jonny's bladder and prostate will be used for testing that will aid thousands of people with bladder and prostate problems.

Over eight hundred people attended the funeral mass for Jonny, and the Billingsleys were amazed at how many lives their son had touched. In his young life, he had made more friends of all ages than even he could have imagined.

Neighborhood friends and high school buddies brought gifts to the accident scene, and it didn't take long to transform the telephone pole on the corner into a small memorial. Teddy bears, flowers, candles, and angels were placed at the site—an affirmation of friendship. This place also served as a place to pray, cry, and heal.

Jonny's friends struggled with his death, and they gathered in his bedroom to talk, cry, and try to make sense out of their incredible loss. One evening, after the kids left, Jonny's parents found a folded-up piece of paper lying on their son's bed. They sat down and read it together. It said, *I know his name will never pop up on my Buddy list again; however, it will remain there forever.*

Throughout his life, Jonathon Billingsley gave his family love and joy. Now, through his death, he brings them pride in his decision to help others. Jonny was unselfish in life, and a part of him now lives on in the recipients of his organs. Maybe someday Jonny's family will meet these people, but for now, his parents are content knowing their teenage son made a better life for others.

# Beautiful, Beautiful Scars

by Jan Kern

GRASS VALLEY, CALIFORNIA

Jackie shuffled into Mike's office wearing her usual black-hooded sweatshirt and plopped down on the middle cushion of the vinyl couch. As Mike swiveled his desk chair toward her, she wondered what this meeting would hold. Since arriving at the residential ministry two months before, she mostly met with John. But he was out of town.

It wasn't that Mike was intimidating. She just didn't know him. She'd seen him around a lot, talked to him a few times. He had even prayed with her. But usually when she saw him she smiled, said hi, and went on.

They began to chat casually about how things were going with the other kids at the ministry. What did she think about the upcoming wilderness trip—was she okay with it? Yeah, that wasn't a problem. Was there anything she wanted to talk about?

Jackie began to share a little about her past, and it somehow led to her telling him straight out, "I'm a cutter." She knew Mike was aware of this fact. He'd read what she wrote about herself when she applied to come to the ministry. He had met with her and her parents when she first came. But this was the first time she'd actually admitted the self-injury to anyone there except John. It surprised her.

The next moments she told more of her story but kept the sleeves of her sweatshirt firmly gripped in her hands. As the meeting went on, she revealed the deep pain she felt inside and the guilt she

Choosing Life

carried from years of being abused. She longed for freedom. Though the meeting was about over, Mike seemed to sense her need for something more.

He said, "I want to close in prayer and bring all of this to Jesus." He paused. "Would you be willing to pull back your sleeves so we can bring your scars to Jesus?"

Jackie's anxiety shot up. No one had ever asked her to reveal her scars, and there were many. They made her feel ugly and she hated everything about them. She didn't like the questions and the stares of others. Any way she could, she avoided explaining. That's why she wore the long sleeves. The story behind the scars was too huge for a simple answer.

And yet . . . she had just shared part of that story with Mike. Could she let *him* see the scars?

She looked at Mike. She could tell he wasn't asking out of curiosity, like she was some freak show. He genuinely cared. Quietly, she slid up both sleeves to reveal forearms slashed with many marks, some of them fresh.

"Jackie, only Jesus can make these scars beautiful," Mike said tenderly. "Only He can give meaning to these scars and bring healing to the hurt that lies behind them. Can we pray for that?"

Jackie looked down at her scars. Make these beautiful? It sounded crazy. Mike went on. He began to talk about Thomas and Jesus.

"Jesus came to save the lost. His bloodstained hands, feet, and side are proof of the death-defying power of His love for us. There is no place His love cannot reach."

Jackie wanted to believe that.

Mike continued, "Jesus told Thomas to put his hands in His

side, to see the wounds in His hands. The wounds of Christ built unshakable confidence in Thomas' heart. His doubts were put to rest as he touched those most beautiful of scars."

Jackie searched Mike's eyes. "Can God really do that? Use my scars and cuts in a beautiful way?"

"Yes," Mike assured her. "We can pray that Jesus' wounds and scars be the healing of yours. Can I pray for that for you?"

Mike wasn't pushing. Jackie knew she could say no and he'd be okay with it, but she always seemed to struggle with pleasing everyone. She partly wanted to say yes just so she wouldn't disappoint him. Mostly she craved the healing he talked about. She finally nodded and they bowed their heads.

"Jesus, make your wounds Jackie's wounds. Make Jackie's wounds full of purpose and meaning, without fear of guilt." Jackie felt Mike's light touch on her arms as he prayed that she would believe Christ's shed blood was sufficient to heal every area of her life. He asked that the scars she hid would become reminders of Jesus' love for her in the days ahead.

He finished and they lifted their heads. Tears streaked both of their faces.

"Jackie, it took great courage to share your scars. Thank you for revealing your pain and letting me pray for you."

She left Mike's office that day with a smile she couldn't hold back. She realized the step she had taken and what it meant. It was a beginning she thought she'd never see, a U-turn from a life of endless pain. For the first time, she felt a sliver of hope. She could get better and overcome the urges to hurt herself. Jesus' wounds and scars were for her, and they held the promise that hers would be healed. They too could become beautiful, beautiful scars.

# The Truth Will Set You Free

by Karen Kosman as told by Priscilla Cruz

LA MIRADA, CALIFORNIA

My nightmare started when I was four and lasted for several years. My abuser was my own cousin. I remember it all, the sexual abuse, him slapping me. Disabled with cerebral palsy, I had trouble speaking and I fell a lot, so my parents never questioned the bruises on my body. Fear kept me from telling. I remember crying inside it hurt so much. I dreaded each time I found myself alone with him. It didn't stop until I was twelve, and only because my abuser moved away. But the fear didn't go away. It stayed inside me and festered like an infected wound. I thought my life was over.

When I was fourteen, I reached a point where my self-hatred and disgrace could no longer be kept inside. I finally chose to tell my school counselor what had happened to me.

She said, "Priscilla, you need to tell your parents and the authorities."

*How could I tell my parents?* I thought.

When my school counselor called my mom in for a conference, she told her I had been molested and the person had moved away.

My parents then arranged for me to see a professional counselor who attended our church. With his help I told my parents the whole story. They were shocked, yet accepting. We cried together. Suddenly counselors, police, and social workers were at my door wanting to know about the abuse. At first I didn't want to tell them anything. I was terrified. I wanted to die. Telling the story over and over made me suicidal.

One day I prayed about the situation, and all of a sudden I felt protected. Although I still felt scared, I finally knew God was with me. He would walk with me through this ordeal. Prayer changed everything for me and drew me close to God. I felt safe knowing He was with me and loved me no matter how damaged I was.

As I waited for the arrest, and then for the trial to begin, I felt life was so unfair.

Once my abuser was arrested, some of my relatives called me a liar—they believed I had made the whole thing up. That hurt me so much. They did not understand how hard it was to tell anyone about that horrible time. Fortunately, my parents stood by me and supported me all the way. But things did not get easier after the arrest.

I developed panic attacks and always felt like I needed to be with my parents. They took me out of public school and homeschooled me for a year. It was hard being away from my friends and people I loved, but the only place I felt safe was at home.

Each morning I debated if it was worth getting out of bed to face another agonizing day. My emotions went up and down like a roller coaster ride. Then one day I got down on my knees and prayed, "God, I'm really upset with you. It feels like you've taken my life away. Why?"

After my prayer I remained on my knees and sobbed before God. Suddenly I realized God, my Father, was sobbing, too. I understood for the first time that God was like my dad, and He was deeply hurt by all the pain I was facing. I was His child. I felt a deep sense of peace and slept through the night for the first time in a long time.

The entire preparation for court seemed to drag on forever. The week before the trial began I cried and prayed alone in my room every day. I had never felt so afraid. Then one morning I woke up and felt God's arms around me. I really don't know how else to explain it. I just knew He would never let my abuser hurt me again. That morning I took the stand and swore to tell the truth and nothing but the truth, so help me God, and He did.

The defense attorney threw questions at me. I thought, *These people aren't nice.*

I remained on the stand for five hours. Telling my story in front of all those people was hard. The cross-examination was so awful, I was sure that hell couldn't be worse. Then the judge said, "Priscilla, we'll need you back in court tomorrow."

*Yeah, right! I'm never coming back,* I thought, scowling.

Yet the next morning I was back on the stand for another three hours of questioning. The judge allowed me to take as many time-outs as I needed. I would either run to the rest room and cry or join my mom and friends in the hallway. I was blessed to have friends who came just to support me.

Later, at home in my room, I prayed, "Father, I don't know if I can stand another day in court."

Then a gentle voice whispered, "The truth will set you free." I began praising God in song and thanking Him for the awesome sense of self-worth He had just given me.

On the last day of court, I went with a new sense of peace. On the stand again, I said everything that needed to be said. When I went home I felt as if I were on cloud nine. It was over, and I just wanted to see justice done.

Justice did not turn out like I thought it would. In a plea bargain, my abuser pleaded guilty to just one of the counts. After he got out of jail he'd have to register as a child molester wherever he lived. It seemed unfair to me. Was this justice? He'd be free to hurt another child.

That night I prayed, "God, I'm angry again. How could you let this happen? You know I told the truth. I just don't understand."

Suddenly I realized that my anger was sin, too. I wasn't God. He knew what He was doing. "Forgive me, Father," I prayed.

Several months have passed since the trial, and I still don't understand the justice system and the decisions made. What I do understand is that without Christ I would not have survived.

None of us has enough strength to face trials in life alone. The good news is God gives us His strength. In our weakness we are made strong in Christ. I guess the bottom line is that Christ is the reason I'm alive. It is through Christ I chose to make a U-turn from hopelessness to wholeness, that I chose life instead of an easier way out. When everything else in life seems to be wrong or against you, turning to Jesus will help you be all right. I know. Just ask me.

Choosing Life

# The Story With No Ending

by D. Marie Hutko

REISTERSTOWN, MARYLAND

The hospital emergency room bustled with activity at around nine o'clock on a school weeknight as my mother and father checked me into triage. I stood between them, my body feeling weaker and weaker, and my eyelids fluttering open and closed.

I could hear the faraway sound of an unrecognizable voice asking question after question of me.

"What did you take?" *Sleeping pills.*

"When did you take them?" *About forty-five minutes ago.*

"How much do you weigh?" *One forty-five.*

"How old are you?" *Sixteen.*

"Are you allergic to any medications?" *No.*

"How many pills did you take?" *About sixty.*

"Sixteen?" *No! Sixty.*

"Oh. You were serious."

Yes, I thought I was. But at that one frantic moment, I wanted so badly for someone to save me.

It was hard for me to understand whether I wanted to be saved because I truly regretted taking the pills, or because I thought it was the right way to act in front of these people who discovered my secret. It was probably a little of both. I was mixed-up.

I do know that what brought me to the ER in the first place was a sign from God that my life was worth living; my mission here on earth was not complete. Why else would my mother have found that one, lone pill that I dropped on the bathroom floor upon my hasty consumption of several packages of sleeping pills?

My mother had shared the Lord with me throughout my life, revealing His presence to me in many ways. That night the Lord revealed himself to me through my mother. He wasn't done with me yet.

After the doctor ordered me to drink liquid charcoal, the nurse inserted a tube in one of my nostrils, then forced it down my esophagus and into my belly. This device siphoned the poison from my stomach. Amidst the bustle of the ER, my alertness ebbed and flowed. During an acute state of awareness, the tube annoyed my face, like something that didn't belong.

I ripped the flexible tubing from my face. Some of the black charcoal splattered across my face and some flew into the air, obstructing my mother's view as a few drops splashed onto her glasses.

"Oh no! Mom . . . I am so sorry . . . I am so sorry!"

Deep inside I was incredibly sorry. Not just for getting her glasses dirty, but for distorting her view of me and our life together. I felt her pain, and it hurt more than my own.

I instinctively began to pray—for my safety, for my family's pain to be eased—and I apologized to God for letting Him down. Was I a hypocrite for now asking for God's help? Or was this the beginning of true repentance?

I wanted God to help me because it sure didn't seem that I could help myself. I felt ashamed. I felt powerless. I felt confused. I depended on the people around me to save me, yet I simultaneously pushed them away. What did it matter anyway? If I died, there would be no more fear, no more feeling, and no more pain.

After the poison was pumped from my stomach, a straw in a cup containing an orange-tasting drink was continuously being pushed

Choosing Life

in front of my mouth. The nurse repeated, "Drink, drink . . . drink some more."

"No," I resisted. "It makes me feel like throwing up."

"That's what we want you to do. Throw up, get all the poison out of your system," said the nurse.

She persisted, and I resisted to no avail. All I wanted was to sleep, but no one would let me. All I wanted was to be left alone, but no one would let me.

The doctor released me from the hospital the next day, after I spoke with a psychiatrist on staff. Once I convinced him that I would see an outside psychologist once a week, and I was not a danger to myself or anyone else, I was free.

I was able to continue with a mostly normal life. After a self-imposed hiatus, I returned to the weekly Sunday church sermons. If I had been the doctor handling my case, I would have prescribed church from the get-go, as well as traditional psychotherapy, because it was there my healing really began.

I felt relieved, but still ashamed. I was happy my attempt was only that—an attempt. I never felt so happy to have failed, but the repercussions of the underlying problem would haunt me for years to come. A never-ending feeling of melancholy shrouded my life at every turn.

I met with my designated psychologist once a week for almost a year. I began the process of appreciating my own self-worth, but the road to discovering and loving oneself can take a long time to travel.

An often-asked question after someone attempts suicide is, *Why did you do it?* I did it because I placed 100 percent of my self-worth in a boy—a teenage boy. When the relationship went sour, I was distraught. That was the quick, easy answer. The more difficult, precise answer revealed itself years later.

I never truly enjoyed much of anything. "Muddling through" is what I used to say when someone asked how I was. I struggled in college. Not with grades, but rather with the ups and downs in everyday life. One of the few ups included church attendance. The Lord lifted me up and renewed me each Sunday, but by the next day, I was down in the dumps again.

My turning point came when I made the choice to consult with a psychiatrist to figure out why most of my life was spent in a perpetual state of melancholy. She diagnosed depression, prescribed an antidepressant, and met with me once a week for three years.

My U-turn began that day. Through medication and therapy, I gained an abundance of insight into who I was, where I had come from, and where I wanted to go. A new "up" in my life was my counseling sessions. I started to love myself.

I began to write more often and realized I was happiest when I wrote. I fancied searching for the truth through my writing and it pleased me to transcribe those journeys to the page for others to read.

Today I am alive and healthy. I continue my prescription for antidepressants and probably will until God is ready to accept me into His kingdom.

My story has no permanent earthly ending, I am happy to say. Each day grants me a new beginning, and I am quite simply thankful.

# Leaving Luggage in France

by Charles Gibson

CENTERVILLE, MINNESOTA

"I need a hand with this suitcase." Andy struggled to move the heavy weight from the trunk of the car to the ground.

"How heavy can it be?" Charles yanked on the handle and the suitcase barely moved. "What's in here, lead weights or a bag of cement?"

"Nope, tools actually." Andy was serious. "I brought hammers, hacksaws, screwdrivers, a cordless drill, tape measures, a tool belt, and duct tape. I want to be ready for any job."

Charles shook his head. "You put all your tools in one suitcase? We have a long walk to the train station." Charles chuckled. "You really haven't traveled much, have you?"

Except for one trip to Canada, Andy had never been outside of the United States. When presented with the opportunity to go to Toulouse, France, on a short-term mission trip, he immediately signed up. Being the only teenager among men on the trip, it took some courage for him to go.

Interested in pursuing construction trades, Andy wanted to help with remodeling a pharmacy into a church building. Since quality tools are very expensive in France, our team of volunteers brought all the necessary tools—just not all stuffed into one suitcase.

Prior to the trip, all the men, including Andy, had met for a pre-trip informational discussion. He was deceptively quiet, but the men learned later that he had no problem being verbal. Upon arrival in France, Andy rattled off words with the tempo of a machine gun.

His statements gave new meaning to the term run-on sentence. The only time he ceased talking was when he strained to pick up his suitcase, which the men noticed was an old tan Samsonite, half-wrapped with duct tape. The case had obviously seen better days, probably years ago.

"What's all the duct tape for?" one of the men asked.

"It wouldn't stay shut any other way," Andy replied. "The latch didn't work right, so I just wrapped a little duct tape around it. That gray tape fixes everything."

While most of the team's luggage could be wheeled around, Andy's was awkward. He carried the suitcase, dragged it, heaved it up on his shoulders, shared his burden with others, and left duct tape residue on several Paris escalators and walkways. Considering the age of the case, it fared quite well through all the jostling about. That tan Samsonite was one tough container. Just like Andy himself.

The men on the team didn't know it then, but Andy had fought his share of battles by the time he turned seventeen. For a period of time in his life, his existence was a yearly report of bad news. His parents legally separated when he was eight. They divorced when he was nine, and his dad disappeared from his life. At the age of ten he was diagnosed with attention deficit disorder (ADD) and prescribed Ritalin. Struggling in school, he was placed in special education classes when he was eleven.

Andy hated his medication, the special education classes, and the label of ADD. He was determined not to let his circumstances define his identity. He resisted taking Ritalin. It was supposed to help him focus, but it slowed his thoughts, leaving him feeling "like a zombie." He slept whenever he could, but when he woke up, he often felt like he was in a daze, unable to concentrate. The Ritalin helped others cope with him, but it didn't touch the pain and abandonment he felt.

Andy was eleven when he came to Christ. After watching movies about the end times at a friend's house, Andy knew he wanted to be ready when the Lord returned. He didn't want to be abandoned by his heavenly Father. Andy's heart had completely changed, but he continued struggling with his identity as a teenager, unsure of what God wanted in his life. On the outside, Andy seemed open and social, but inside, he was still emotionally closed. It seemed this mission trip was the catalyst he hoped would define his identity in Christ.

"How are you going to open that suitcase?" One of the men knew how difficult it was to remove duct tape once it was placed.

"I don't know." Andy contemplated the situation. "Got any scissors?"

As Andy tried to hack the tape of his Samsonite using a pen, keys, his teeth, and anything else he could find, he took a step back and said, "Duct tape sure keeps a suitcase closed. It's gone halfway around the world and I still can't get it off. If I could only get my saw out, I could cut a hole in this thing. But I guess that wouldn't work, either. I couldn't get all my stuff back home with a hole in the suitcase. Maybe I could cover the hole with duct tape. Wait, here's a pair of scissors." Andy started tackling the tape. "Things are sure a lot easier to open if they're not wrapped so tight." The other missionary, Charles, just shook his head and laughed.

Andy and Charles stayed with a family in Toulouse. After long days of construction work, they had many late-night conversations, and Andy began opening up about his struggles and owning his own beliefs.

One thing he had no trouble owning was his part of the work. He teamed with Charles most of the week, knocking down walls and constructing new ones. Andy's endless chatter disappeared as he focused on the job in front of him. In spite of problems with power tools, Andy eagerly worked, even with handheld screwdrivers. Instead of being a distraction, Andy kept their project moving.

"It feels like I get a better look at the world from here," Andy shared with Charles one night. "I think I can see myself the way God sees me and not just the way everyone else sees me. A lot of people told me what I should believe about God, but I never got it. Now that I'm so far from home, I think I can see what really matters. It's what God says I should think about myself. I don't have to always please others to please Him."

A couple days later, the team packed up to return home, and everyone was looking for Andy's duct-taped Samsonite.

"Where's the lead weight?" Charles asked.

"In the trash, where it belongs," Andy smiled as he related his story of how he left all his tools with the new church and tossed the weary case. "They need them more than I do."

"Even the duct tape?" Charles asked.

"Especially the duct tape."

The whole team agreed that Andy left more behind in France than just an old suitcase and a bunch of tools. On the way home he didn't seem as intense or anxious. He sat peacefully without fidgeting and talking constantly. Duct tape can hold a suitcase closed, much like Andy was able to close himself emotionally. But like the tools inside the case, unless you open the cover, they're of no use.

Something happened to Andy during that mission trip. In spite of his fears, he had taken a risk and opened himself up to a new experience. God honored that decision and used Andy's time in France to give him a greater sense of his identity in Christ.

God created everyone for a purpose. Paul wrote to the Philippians that we must each "continue to work out your salvation with fear and trembling." We are all wired differently, yet God has marked us as His own. Our identity comes from Him. Like Andy, if we know Christ, we are not primarily ADD, anxious, overweight, anorexic, depressed, athletic, popular, or gifted. We are all God's children.

# The Cop That God Sent

by Karen Kosman

LA MIRADA, CALIFORNIA

That summer my parents lost their full-time baby-sitter. At fourteen, I took over the responsibility of my younger brothers and sister. The summer days were exceptionally hot. One day, as I noticed the police officer directing heavy traffic from the nearby horse races, I felt compelled to take him an ice-cold glass of juice. I found out his name was Bill, and his warm smile made me feel like I'd known him for a lifetime. I learned he was married and had two children. Number three was on the way. Somehow I knew he was a good dad.

He loved to tease me, and after a few repeat visits he told me, "You know, Karen, fights have broken out at the police department. Officers are fighting over whose turn it is to be stationed on this corner where a gracious young teenager serves cold drinks with a smile."

Finally the day arrived when Officer Bill was no longer stationed at our corner, and I really missed our chats. He had become kind of like a father to me.

A few weeks later, a stranger came to our door, posing as a contractor. He had personal information that convinced me he had been hired by my dad. I allowed him into the house, but when he got me alone he grabbed me from behind. I felt a knife blade against my throat as he said, "Don't scream or I'll kill you." A ripple of terror shot through my whole body. The rapist stole my innocence and left behind a shadow of fear that seemed to attach itself to my soul.

After he left, I escaped to a neighbor's home with my sister and

Choosing Life

brothers at my side, where my parents and the police were called. That afternoon, I longed to be my daddy's little girl once more, to have him hold me and tell me that I'd be all right. When he learned I'd been raped, he turned and walked away from me. The foundation of my world crumbled.

When the police questioned me, I felt more like a criminal than a victim. My parents had their own pain and were unable to meet my needs. I felt alone and abandoned.

The day Mom called me to talk with two detectives I had reached the bottom of my despair. Suicidal thoughts plagued me. It was with a reluctant heart that I entered the room where two men waited for me. I lowered my head as I sat on a dining room chair. My hands were clasped so tightly they ached. Inside I screamed, *Don't they know each time I repeat my story, it's like being tortured again?* My thoughts were interrupted when I heard a familiar voice say, "Karen, do you remember me?"

When I looked up, I saw the deep blue eyes of my policeman friend, Officer Bill. He gently placed his hands over mine and said, "This terrible thing was not your fault. It's okay to cry." Tears I'd kept locked up finally escaped.

At that moment, God allowed a U-turn in my life—one that turned me around from a path of discouragement and suicidal thoughts. Through the help of this special policeman, God placed me on a path of hope and gave me a spirit of renewal.

In addition to the help my friend Bill offered, I started attending a local church and soon committed my life to Christ. As I grew in my faith I saw clearly how God's providence had been at work. Bill had been promoted to detective and assigned to my case. In time, he became a surrogate dad to me. I knew God had arranged a U-turn in my life, with this special fatherly policeman as my guide.

On his days off or after work, Officer Bill often stopped by my house and sat at our kitchen table, talking with Mom and me. He introduced me to his wife, Helen, who welcomed me. Their home became a safe harbor for me, where unconditional love continued to help me heal. God knew I would need some special friends to survive. God reached out to me and as I reached back to Him, He provided for everything I would need to survive being raped. God took the evil that invaded my life and used it to His glory.

Yes, it's true that God allows U-turns, but sometimes He sends people to help show us the way. I am so thankful God provided a policeman to help me change my direction.

# chooeing to witness

*Then he said: "The God of our fathers has chosen you to know his will and to see the Righteous One and to hear words from his mouth. You will be his witness to all men of what you have seen and heard. And now what are you waiting for? Get up, be baptized and wash your sins away, calling on his name."* —Acts 22:14-16

Sometimes people say we have to go to seminary or memorize the whole Bible or pray for hours before we can be a true witness for Jesus. So how come when someone is a witness in court they don't have to go to school or read special books to tell a group of people what they've experienced? Telling of their experiences is what a witness does. A witness for Jesus simply tells how God has changed their life; in other words, they tell what they have experienced. Can we share what we know? What we've seen, felt, learned? Then we can be a witness, too. What are we waiting for?

# Kaleidoscope

by Joyce Stark

MONTROSE, SCOTLAND

Jake McGhie worked for the soft drinks bottling plant since he was seventeen. He also pursued his hobby of painting.

Jake painted primarily scenes of small towns. His main concern was color. When he saved enough money, he attended art classes in the nearby city of Aberdeen, Scotland. His teachers quickly recognized Jake's talent. They told him, however, that he needed to moderate his use of colors.

Tall and handsome, Jake was also shy and modest. It surprised his parents and friends when he continued to ignore his teachers' advice.

When he turned thirty-four, he got a phone call from a gallery in Barcelona, Spain. Someone had seen some of his paintings and wanted to act as his Spanish agent. From that one call, everything changed. Jake prospered, stopped working at the bottling plant, and bought a small studio.

Jake adored children. He kept his studio door open, and the local children were welcome to chat with him and watch him paint.

When she was only five, young Lorna became fascinated with watching Jake create his lovely scenes, but by the time she was seventeen, she saw things differently. Everything was factual to her. If you couldn't explain it, it didn't exist. She and Jake had their greatest arguments about God and beliefs.

"You sound so cynical," Jake told her one afternoon. "Proof of God is everywhere, in every flower that blooms, in every sunset. You just don't see it."

The young woman studied him and sighed. "Nature is fine, but the world is full of things that you've never encountered because you're tucked away here in your studio. You never ask the kinds of questions I do. You just have a blind faith. I need more explanation than that," she said irritably.

When Jake didn't respond she accused, "You are the least inquisitive man I know."

Jake smiled and explained, "When I was ten I was the most inquisitive boy anyone could know. I had to investigate everything, even areas where people would tell me not to meddle."

Jake shook his head at his memories and continued, "I was always fascinated by colors, and my prized possession one Christmas was a kaleidoscope. I can see it to this day, made of metal and painted in bright colors. I used to turn it all day long and sit up half the night with the light on, marveling at all the wonderful patterns unfolding in front of me.

"Unfortunately, that was not enough for my inquisitive mind. I had to see how it worked, what made all the wonderful patterns, so I tried to unscrew it. My mum warned me I would spoil it forever. But I chose to ignore her, and when she was out, I took a knife and pried open the end of the kaleidoscope that held everything in place. You know what happened?"

Lorna shook her head, "No, what?"

"Little pieces of cheap plastic and mirrored glass fell on the table. My kaleidoscope of a million patterns lay there, and it could never be repaired, could never give me all that pleasure again. I cried almost immediately, because I knew what I had done. It was as if I had killed something very close to me, Lorna. I could not forgive myself for choosing to do such a senseless act. I started to paint the next day. I have spent my life trying to put back the colors I so carelessly wiped out.

"I learned never to try analyzing something of great beauty, but instead to accept it for what it is," he continued. "I learned that if you try to uncover the magic behind something, you will destroy the magic itself. You are young and intelligent, and there is so much you want to find out. But be careful. Don't demand proof from the Lord that He exists. Don't apply your cold reasoning to every single miracle He performs every day of your life. Open your heart as well as your eyes, Lorna. Don't cut open the kaleidoscope. You will be left with nothing but little bits of plastic."

Tears streamed down Lorna's cheeks and she let out a sob. She threw herself into Jake's open arms and confessed, "I am so lost. I feel so completely alone. I am scared to look into your kaleidoscope in case I see nothing but black and white, in case I do not deserve to see the colors you see!"

Jake smiled as he soothed her. "Trust in the Lord. Simply believe in Him and ask Him to help you. He will surround you with color. He already does; you just don't see it yet!"

Lorna went off to college the next week. She wrote to Jake a couple of times each month. She made new friends, went to church regularly, and met a wonderful young man. Jake was pleased at all of her news, but what pleased him most was a note he got from her about six months after their discussion in his studio:

*My dearest Jake,*
*I just had to drop you a note to tell you that something amazing*

*happened to me. I was saying a little prayer this morning. I looked up, and outside my window was the most vivid rainbow I have ever seen. I realized the Lord was showing me that my kaleidoscope was still intact. I hadn't managed to cut it open and I wouldn't be left with the bits of plastic.*

*Thank you.*
*Love, Lorna*

# Accepting Without Understanding

by Shelley Wake

ABERGLASSLYN, NEW SOUTH WALES, AUSTRALIA

One day my mother came home from a parent-teacher meeting and told me that since I was such a good English student, it would be nice if I helped someone else in my class.

"All right," I said, "that sounds good. I would like to help."

"Great. Robbie will come over every Wednesday."

"Robbie? Mom, you can't be serious!"

"Oh, yes, I am." She smiled.

Mom was an inspiration. She helped so many people it left me speechless. When things happened she was always the first to offer help. And it didn't have to be a tragedy. She reached out to anyone she thought needed help. I was always proud of her and tried to do my part . . . except when it interfered with my life. Then I wasn't so happy about it.

Robbie was not a good person. He was always in trouble. He was mean to everyone. He was no good at school. And I was terrified about what my friends would think of me.

*What if they think Robbie and I are friends? What if they think he is my boyfriend? How will I ever live that down?*

I begged Mom not to make me tutor him. I told her it was unfair. I told her Robbie wasn't worthy of help.

Mom shook her head slowly when I said that. Then she said gently, "Darling, our place is not to judge who is worthy of help. Our place is to help everyone we can, in whatever way we can. God is the only judge."

God Allows U-Turns for Teens                    152

"But you should see what Robbie is like in class!" I rationalized. "He doesn't listen, he's always in trouble. He doesn't even want to be helped."

"You don't know that, darling. You don't know anything about him."

She was right. I didn't know anything about him. I knew what I saw, but I knew nothing of the reasons why. My mother told me there was a reason why Robbie did the things he did. She said she would not tell me that reason, because it was not the point. The point was that we don't have to know the reasons to offer help.

Mom said there was only one rule to use in deciding whether or not to help people, one question to ask.

"Can you help?" She looked me in the eyes.

Of course I could help Robbie.

"Then there is no reason why you shouldn't."

I accepted what she said and became Robbie's homework partner. Every Wednesday he turned up on time. The Robbie who came to my home wasn't the same Robbie who came to class. In class he was loud, always talking and making smart comments. The Robbie who came to my place was polite, even a little shy.

I didn't talk to Robbie much about his life. I never learned why he acted the way he did in class. But I did learn his grades improved. And I noticed as the grades began to improve, he began to behave better in class.

Friends asked me why Robbie came to my house every week. They wondered if he and I were friends.

"Yes," I told them, "we are friends."

Robbie and I didn't stay in touch after we graduated. I don't know what he made of his life, but I know he got into college. And I remember how proud he looked the day he graduated from high school. He wasn't the top graduating student, but I think he may have been the happiest.

Initially, Robbie didn't seem like the right kind of friend to have, but I learned in God's eyes he was as worthy of my friendship as anyone else. Everyone deserves the hand of friendship, which doesn't always mean understanding. I guess that's what witnessing really means, you know? Sometimes witnessing may even mean helping.

Whether or not we offer that help is a choice we all need to make. It's a U-turn that changed my life—and Robbie's.

# Just Different Enough

by Sandra McGarrity

CHESAPEAKE, VIRGINIA

What was it with that girl? Why did she always have that big smile plastered across her face? Why did she walk with a cheerful bounce in her step? Why did she speak to everyone she met? Why was she so happy? Why was she different from most of the teenagers that I knew? Why?

That girl had a definite mystery about her. She cheered me and infuriated me. She drew me and repelled me. On some days I was puzzled by her behavior, and on other days I knew for certain she couldn't be in her right mind. I didn't understand her at all.

What in the world did she have to be so very happy about? She wasn't anything special. I mean, she wasn't even popular. How could a teenage girl be that happy when she wasn't even popular?

She wasn't ugly or anything, but she hadn't won any beauty contests and she hadn't ever been the homecoming queen. She wasn't dumb, but she wasn't valedictorian of her class. She wasn't rich with designer clothes and driving around in some hot little sports car her dad had bought her. She wasn't a star athlete and didn't date one, either. Duh, she didn't even have a boyfriend!

I would meet her in the halls of the tech school we were attending, and she would smile her happy smile, always, without fail. The smile made me feel happy for a few minutes, then puzzled. My mind had conversations with her while my face smiled back. *Stop smiling! Look angry or look sad! Don't look happy! You are a teenager with none of the required things to make a teenager happy, so quit being happy,*

Choosing to Witness

*already!* I kind of wanted to catch her in a sour mood, but it never happened.

Maybe the reason she bugged me so much was because I was a teenager too, with none of the required things to make me happy, either. As a matter of fact, as a person fighting daily to be as normal as the other kids, I had even less of the required things. That was my opinion, anyway. *I* didn't go around smiling like I lived in Mister Rogers' neighborhood.

I knew her name, and that was about all I knew about her. She was a year older than I, but I had seen her around. We had gone to the same church until I stopped going. Over the weeks, I decided I had to get to know her. I needed to figure out what was wrong with her.

We didn't have the same classes, but I could slip out to the rest room whenever I pleased. So when the architecture class went on a break, I strolled out of the business classroom. As I expected, she was sitting in the lounge area of the rest room. We exchanged some polite small talk while I washed my hands.

In the days ahead, we began to talk more and more. I found out things weren't always good in her life and she didn't try to hide the fact, but she was never discouraged or angry. She often spoke of church activities, so I began to suspect that her "religion" had something to do with her attitude.

One day as we talked, I blurted, "Why are you always so happy?"

That big smile spread across her face and she answered, "I'm not always happy. The problems just don't get me down so bad because I know I'm going to heaven one day and all of my problems will be over."

I nodded my head to show that I understood, but I really didn't. My mind was a jumble of thoughts. Wasn't she being a little presumptuous to say she *knew* she was going to heaven? Did she think she was *that* good? I immediately rejected that idea. By now, I knew this girl and there was no way she thought she was better than anyone else was. But how could she be so sure?

I waited a few days before I brought up the subject again. During one of our "rest room talks" I asked, "How is it you say you *know* you are going to heaven?"

She patiently explained, "Jesus died for my sins so I wouldn't have to pay for them. I know I am going to heaven because I have accepted what He did for me."

I still didn't really get it, but she didn't push. She started bringing books for me to read. She asked me to attend Sunday evening church services with her, and I did. She bought me a new Bible in which she wrote I was her "dearest friend, second only to Jesus Christ."

She completed her training and took a job in another city. I quit going to church again. Before long, I finished my training, got married, and moved out of state. We lost touch, but I didn't forget the things she had shown me.

Because of my experience with this girl, I wanted deeply to go to church. My new husband was more than willing to go with me. More seeds were planted and watered in our hearts at church and through people that came our way. We both chose to accept Christ as our Savior after nearly a year of marriage.

It took a while for me to come to Christ. It didn't happen the first time I heard the gospel. God used what some people would call an oxymoron: a happy and contented teenager. Thank you, my friend, for being just different enough to catch my attention.

# Six Months to Live

by Eva Allen
BLOOMINGTON, INDIANA

"You have six months to live" is not a well-received prognosis, especially if you are fifteen years old. We were sophomores in high school when my best friend, Amy, was diagnosed with liver cancer. When doctors discovered it, the cancer had already invaded 75 percent of her body. How could this happen to someone so young? It wasn't fair. Cancer only hits people we don't know, and it definitely doesn't affect teenagers, does it?

Our school was in total shock as we watched Amy undergo chemotherapy treatments and lose her beautiful, midnight-black hair. Dark circles grew larger beneath her sinking eyes. Her deteriorating body shriveled to a meager eighty-two pounds. Soon her classmates had to push her to class in a wheelchair. Seeing her condition worsen every day sent most of us home crying and questioning God.

Then, one spring day, Amy didn't show up to be wheeled to class. She had fallen asleep the night before and did not wake up. We honestly thought Amy would get better. We should have been prepared for this day, yet somehow we weren't ready at all.

The entire school shut down for Amy's funeral. We walked silently across the street in the drizzling rain to a little stone church to say good-bye. Everyone was in a daze. There were so many tears, so many questions, and so many broken hearts. Our spirits were crushed. We were torn and confused.

After the service concluded, several youth ministers and teachers gathered groups of students together to talk over everything we were experiencing. What began as a huge ocean of angry and hurtful tears flowed into a season of prayer and ultimately led to a number of our classmates giving their lives to Christ.

One of those students was a friend of mine named Jason. Jason had recently been dealing with some tough times and was contemplating suicide. That day something was revealed to him through Amy's death. Amy had found joy and safety in the strong arms of God long before her body developed cancer. Everyone knew of her faith and trust in the Lord, even when her situation seemed entirely hopeless. Jason saw that hope in her, and through it found peace for his life, too. His life took a dramatic U-turn that day. Not only did Jason find a reason to live, he later became a youth minister who guided many more teenagers like him to find safety in the arms of a loving God.

As for me, I learned two things from Amy. First, I realized each day should be treated like a robin's egg. This little blue speckled egg houses the potential to grow a beautiful creature, yet it is also incredibly delicate and easily broken. I have chosen to cherish today, to enjoy my friends more, to tell people I love them more often, and to hang out with God more.

Secondly, I discovered we are all being watched. Not in the sense that aliens on some distant planet are studying our every move, but when we have faith in God, people around us will observe the way we live—from the way we speak to a scrawny, awkward freshman, to how we handle a great big D in chemistry class. God asks us to live by a standard that might seem odd to the onlooker, but what if Amy had chosen to compromise or ditch her faith? Would her death have made as much of an impact on our school? Would students have been on their knees, praying, at her funeral? Would Jason have found Jesus? I don't know for sure, but I can tell you I'm thankful for Amy's witnessing.

It caused many of us to choose to take our relationship with God much more seriously.

# A Casual Witness

by Esther M. Bailey as told by Matt Lutz
PHOENIX, ARIZONA

Chris, Joey, and Jason were my new high school friends. I'd been hanging around Christians for most of my life, so this friendship with non-Christians was new to me. These guys seemed to have their heads on straight, though, so I decided it was okay to step out of my circle.

When I said yes to a Friday-night sleepover, I didn't exactly have sharing my faith in mind. I merely wanted to have fun with three cool guys.

The evening got off to a trouble-free start: plenty of pop to guzzle, pizza to scarf, and jokes to tell, followed by an intense Nintendo challenge. I was having a blast.

But the moment Jason's parents headed off to a movie, the good, clean fun came to a halt, and trouble raised its ugly head. Jason dragged out one of his dad's adult soft-porn magazines, held it up, and grinned. "Okay, gentlemen," he said, "it's time for some real fun."

Chris and Joey tried to act cool, but they seemed a little edgy, too. My heart skipped a few beats and my hands began to feel clammy. I knew I had to take a stand. I wasn't afraid of being cut down. I figured I might as well find out if the guys were true friends.

"Jason, I'm not so sure this is right," I said. Actually, I was positive the magazine was off limits, but I didn't want to come on too strong.

"It's okay, Matt—it's no big deal," Jason said. "I look at this stuff all the time."

"Don't worry. We won't tell," Joey added.

I slumped back on the couch, wondering how to explain. "It isn't that," I finally said. "I don't want to fill my head with that kind of stuff."

The guys' strange expressions were filled with a million questions, so I sat up and continued. "Sure, looking at pictures like that seems fun, because sex is fun. But we've got to be careful if we don't want to get messed up for life."

The room grew still and the guys just stared in disbelief. "I think it'd be better if I don't stay," I said as I jumped to my feet. "I'll call my mom to come get me."

When I dialed our number from the phone in the kitchen, I got a busy signal. I tried a few more times and gave up. I peeked into the family room, expecting the guys to still be paging through the magazine, but it was nowhere in sight and the guys seemed to be in a serious mood.

Jason met me in the doorway with a soda. "Matt, we've been talking," he said with a red face. "We don't want you to leave. Okay?"

Chris chimed in. "Yeah, we're sorry. We didn't mean to make you feel uncomfortable."

"Let's just forget what happened and get on with the fun," Joey said as he looked down at the floor.

I glanced around to meet each face with a smile. "Deal."

We all jumped into another action-packed Nintendo challenge, but the mood wasn't crazy like before. Everyone was still a bit edgy. Just when I was about to crack a joke to put some life back into the party, Chris spoke up. "I don't get it," he said. "What is it that makes you so—you know—different?"

Yipes! That question had only one answer. I gulped and plunged right in. "I'm a Christian," I said.

As I tried to explain my faith, I soon found myself in a deep discussion about Christianity—deeper than I cared for it to be.

"Would you happen to have a Bible in the house?" I asked.

Jason pulled out a dusty old Bible that was hidden at the back of a shelf. I didn't know quite where to begin, but I did the best I could to explain the miraculous birth of Jesus and why He died on the cross.

"Being a Christian isn't just following a set of rules," I said. "It's having a relationship with Jesus. That happens when you ask Jesus to forgive your sins and turn your life over to Him."

Before long, the time seemed right to ask the ultimate question: "Would you guys like to accept Jesus as your Savior?"

All three nodded. I asked them to stand in a circle and hold hands. I explained how they should pray and then led them. I suggested they pray in their own words. Joey did.

After the prayer, Joey said, "Matt, it was really weird. Before we prayed, I seemed to be under a lot of pressure. But when I asked God to forgive my sins, it felt like a heavy load fell off my shoulders."

Wow! I wondered if I was in an un-churched home or at a testimony meeting. I had heard others say things like that, but I was so young when I asked Jesus to come into my heart that I hadn't felt the load of sin being lifted.

The experience of leading my friends to Christ was absolutely awesome! I couldn't believe how everything happened so naturally. Because I chose to be a witness for the Lord and did not run from the opportunity, three young guys—my peers—made a U-turn toward God and discovered the power of being saved. Not bad for a Friday night sleepover, huh?

# The Help-Wanted Ad in the Bible

by Sharon Dunn

BOZEMAN, MONTANA

I became a Christian in high school, and a misfit named Ricky was a big influence in my decision. Ricky would never have been on the cover of GQ magazine. His dark, greasy hair, combed to one side, was already showing signs of male pattern baldness. Despite his effort and combing, little sprigs stuck out defiantly. Ricky's front teeth touched his lower lips even when his mouth was closed. He wore glasses and was four-foot-nothing. As if nature hadn't stacked the cards against him, he walked around the school carrying a Bible.

Although he was not part of the tight drama group I hung out with, he sometimes sat at our table during lunch. When Ricky was out of earshot, we often referred to him as "Greasy Ricky." One afternoon the rest of my friends filtered away, and I was left at the table to finish my burrito with Ricky.

Suddenly Ricky opened his Bible and said, "I've wanted to talk to you for a long time."

I don't remember what he read to me. I do remember he said he was doing this because he cared about me. I made some halfhearted argument and laughed the moment off. But the truth was Ricky's courage floored me. He probably knew he risked even more teasing by sharing the Word of God with me.

In the high school I went to, I suppose there were athletes and honor students who loved Jesus. But they never took the time to talk to me. Ricky did.

If you are waiting until you are perfect or have accomplished something great, thinking that achievement will be your forum for

Choosing to Witness

witnessing, think again. It is not your perfection that will draw people to the gospel; it is Jesus' flawlessness that changes lives.

If God ran a want ad for evangelists, how do you suppose it would read? What sort of qualifications would He be looking for? A good education, connections with the right people, a family with a good reputation? First Corinthians 1:26–28 gives a hint as to the kind of people God wants to use to spread His gospel. He lists four qualifications: First, you do not need to be considered wise by human standards. Second, you need not have influence in the world. Third, God is looking for a few good people, and He doesn't seem to think ancestry and family reputation are important. Finally, even if you are weak and despised, God wants you to work for Him.

Read the want ad in 1 Corinthians. You are qualified right now to change your world for Christ, just like Ricky did.

# A Father's Love

by Michael T. Powers
JANESVILLE, WISCONSIN

His name was Brian, and he was a student at the small high school I attended. Brian was a special education student, suffering from a mild form of retardation, who constantly searched for love and attention, but it usually came for the wrong reasons. Students who wanted to have some "fun" would ask, "Brian, are you the Incredible Hulk?" He would then run down the halls roaring and flexing. He was the joke of the school and was "entertainment" for those who watched. Brian, who was looking for acceptance, didn't realize that they were laughing *at* him and not *with* him.

One day I couldn't take it anymore. I told the other students I had had enough of their game and to knock it off.

"Aw, come on, Mike! We are just having fun. Who do you think you are, anyway?"

The teasing didn't stop for long, but Brian latched on to me that day. I had stuck up for him, and now he was my buddy. Thoughts of *What will people think of you if you are friends with Brian?* swirled in my head, but I forced them out as I realized God wanted me to treat this young man as I would want to be treated.

Later that week I invited Brian over to my house to play video games. Pretty soon he started asking me questions like, "Hey, Mike. Where do you go to church?" I would politely answer his questions, then turn my concentration back to the video game. He kept asking me questions about God, and why I was different from some of the kids at school. Finally Kristi, my girlfriend, pulled me aside and said, "Michael, he needs to talk. How about the two of you go down to your room where you can talk privately?" My wonderfully perceptive future wife had picked up on the cues better than I had.

As soon as we arrived in my room, Brian asked again, "Hey, Mike. How come you're not like some of the other kids at school?"

I knew I needed to tell him about the difference God had made in my life. I got out my Bible and shared John 3:16 and some verses in Romans with him. I explained that God loved him just the way he was, and He had sent Jesus down to earth to die on a cross, rise from the dead, and make it possible for everyone, especially Brian, to spend eternity in heaven if they believed. I didn't know if he comprehended what I was telling him, but when I finished explaining, I asked Brian if he wanted to pray with me. He said he would like that.

We prayed together: "God, I know I am a sinner, but even if I were the only person on earth, I know that you would still have sent your Son down to die on the cross for me and take my place. I accept the gift of salvation you offer, and I ask you to come into my heart and take control. Thank you, Lord. Amen."

I looked at him and said, "Brian, if you meant those words you just prayed, where is Jesus right now?"

He pointed to his heart and said, "He's in here now."

Then he did something I will never forget as long as I live. Brian hugged the Bible to his chest, lay down on the bed, and let the tears flow down the side of his cheeks. When I cry, my sobbing is very loud, but Brian's was unearthly silent as the emotions he'd held inside let loose.

Then he said to me, "Mike, do you know the love God has for

me must be like the love a husband has for his wife or a father has for a son?"

I was floored. Here was someone who had trouble comprehending things in school but had now understood one of eternity's great truths. I now knew he understood what I had shared with him.

He lay there for another five minutes or so as the salty drops continued to flow. I still remember the incredible feeling I had at that moment: a high higher than anything a substance could ever give—the high of knowing God still works miracles in everyday life. John 10:10 immediately came to mind: "I have come that they may have life, and have it to the full."

About a week later everything came into perspective for me. It was then Brian really opened up to me. He explained that his dad had left him and his mom when he was five years old. As Brian stood on the porch that day, his dad told him he was leaving because he couldn't deal with having a son like Brian anymore. Then he walked out of Brian's life and was never seen again. . . . Brian told me he had been looking for his dad ever since. Now I knew why the tears kept flowing that day in my bedroom. His search was over. He found what he had been looking for since he was five years old, a Father's love.

# Boomerang Blessings

by Esther M. Bailey as told by Amber Egelston

SCOTTSDALE, ARIZONA

Every summer since I started high school, I've gone on a short-term mission trip. As worthwhile as these experiences have been, I have gained equal value from the fund-raising efforts to pay for the trips.

After a couple years of sponsoring car washes and soliciting money from friends and family, our youth leader came up with a new twist. He put a brightly colored flyer in the church bulletin that read *RENT-A-KID*. The names of about twenty kids were listed with phone numbers and services offered.

I was open to do most anything, but I included baby-sitting, housework, and cooking on my list. While wondering what results I might get, I received a call.

"Amber, I don't have any jobs for you, but I do have a proposal. If I give you a check for a hundred dollars, would you like to work it out by doing good deeds for people who can't afford to pay?"

Cool, I thought, as an idea already began to form in my mind. "How much work should I do?"

My sponsor said, "I'll leave that entirely up to you."

"I'll get started on it right away," I said.

Through contacts in my church, I knew about a family in real need of help. The husband is paralyzed from the waist down and his general health is poor. His wife works outside the home in addition to caring for their three children. On three occasions I volunteered my services to watch the kids and tidy up the house.

One time I worked for eleven hours straight. The job was quite challenging, especially when the kids got really wild. Some of those hours seemed to crawl! Each time I finished the task, though, I felt fulfilled and very good about myself. Their expressions of appreciation really touched my heart.

By this time I figured I had more than earned the hundred dollars at the normal baby-sitting rate. I wanted to go the extra mile, though, so I was open to yet another opportunity for community service.

Through an outreach ministry of our youth group, I spent a Saturday morning painting over graffiti on the walls of a local residential area. I didn't find the job to be taxing at all. Having my friends working with me, it was almost fun! The families appreciated our help so much, it made up for the clothes I ruined—my fault anyway. Next time I'll wear something old.

After I returned from the mission trip to Mexico, I think the desire to do community service was in my blood. Through the Christian school I attended, I volunteered to help with a party for impoverished children. A lot of planning went into the event: calling for donations, ordering items, last-minute shopping, and many little details that had to be taken care of.

At the party I was in charge of a little girl named Kylee. We played games, decorated cookies, ate pizza, and had some very interesting talks. We really clicked, and people even told us we looked like sisters. This experience was so very rewarding for me. Watching the joy on the children's faces and their excitement over the littlest things humbled me. I cherished the time with the kids, and I've kept Kylee's name tag in my room to pray for her as often as I can.

When my school planned a service trip to a poor church in Mexico, I made the choice to go along. It was a choice that truly did change the story of my life. We took food, money, household goods, and basic supplies to them. During the weekend, our group conducted two church services, prepared two meals for members of the congregation, chopped firewood, painted one of the buildings, and drove their trash to the dump. Any sacrifice I made was more than made up through fellowship with the other students and with members of the congregation. It truly amazed me to see how happy they are with so little.

All of these experiences and more have helped me make a commitment to expand my time in service to the community. I truly enjoy helping people, but it seems I get the best deal. The blessings I hope to bring to others always bounce back to me. Just like a boomerang!

# An Ordinary Kid

by Rebekah Hamrick

FAYETTEVILLE, NORTH CAROLINA

Jeremy was an ordinary kid who spent most of his time playing football and hanging out with his friends. Unfortunately, Jeremy's home situation was not so ordinary. Jeremy's mom and stepdad were alcoholics.

"I can remember time after time, seeing my stepdad beat my mom, sometimes sending her to the hospital. I remember crying and screaming for him to stop hitting her. I was helpless, terrified, and confused," Jeremy recalls.

One hundred miles separated Jeremy from his biological father. Jeremy always looked forward to the time he spent with his dad. They would ride bikes at the park and cook hot dogs outside. Occasionally Jeremy and his brothers slept over at their dad's house. But transportation problems made it difficult for them to get together regularly. During good times, Jeremy and his three brothers saw their father twice a month.

Things continued to get worse at home. One night Jeremy's stepdad hit his mother and busted her lip open. Blood poured down her face and neck.

"I thought I was dreaming," Jeremy said. "I couldn't believe what I was seeing and I couldn't do a thing to stop it!"

No longer able to handle the violence in his home, thirteen-year-old Jeremy talked his mom into letting him move in with his biological father.

"It was hard to leave my mom and brothers, but I had to get away," Jeremy says.

Shortly after moving in with his father, Jeremy began to read a Bible his aunt had given him.

"I was curious about what happened to people when they die. I wasn't satisfied with the answers my mom had given me. I needed to know, and I hoped the Bible would tell me."

Late one night, Jeremy's father, who is a Christian, read from the Bible and showed Jeremy how he could have a home in heaven. It was the U-turn in his life that Jeremy was so desperately seeking.

They prayed together, "Jesus, I know I'm a sinner and I need you to get to heaven. I don't want to go to hell. Please come into my heart and save me from my sins, and forgive me of them. I ask you in your name. Amen."

"It was as if a truckload of guilt and pain was lifted off me! It was the best feeling I have ever had," Jeremy recalls.

It's been six years since Jeremy asked Jesus to be His savior. He admits that it hasn't been an easy road.

"At first I read the Bible a lot and started caring about people more. I was more obedient. Things were going good for a while, but then I went through a spiritual dry spell. I was cussing, watching bad movies, and stuff like that. Then the Lord, always allowing us to make a U-turn in our lives, brought me back to Him. He gave me an increased love for people."

God changed Jeremy's heart and gave him a love for lost souls. It is amazing what the Lord can do if you choose to follow Him.

# choosing to triumph

*Praise be to the God and Father of our Lord Jesus Christ! In his great mercy he has given us new birth into a living hope through the resurrection of Jesus Christ from the dead, and into an inheritance that can never perish, spoil or fade—kept in heaven for you.*

—1 Peter 1:3–4

New birth, living hope, endurable inheritance—all for us! How much God loves us. How much He has in store for us. We are His children. That makes us royalty; did you know that? We are children of the King. What can we do, conquer, establish when we know God has put the dream in our heart? If God is for us, who can be against us? We must grab hold of the vision God casts before us. Step out in the knowledge that He loves us and has plans for us—plans to prosper us and give us hope. We belong to the Creator of the universe. We must step up triumphantly and live like it!

# Proud to Be Me

by Tyrice Harrell
NEW YORK, NEW YORK

My thirteen-year-old cousin, Shaun, a straight-A student with perfect attendance, told me his friends had convinced him to cut school. It was only one day and all the cool kids were doing it, he said. He told me how one of the boys teased him, "Don't be a punk. Nothing is going to happen, you little mama's boy."

These words were so familiar to me. I knew exactly how Shaun felt. Growing up in Brooklyn was tough. By the time I got to junior high school I really felt out of place. I was different, I wasn't hip, I didn't have the designer clothes and the bad attitude, and I couldn't get girls. When the guys my age got into smoking weed and having sex, I was too busy trying to save the princess in Super Mario Bros. I was what they called a goody-two-shoes. Sadly, on my block it wasn't exactly the way to earn cool points. You were only acknowledged if you were doing something rebellious like Darrell, who lived across the street. Everybody knew Darrell. He disrespected his parents, was tough, and ruled the block. I really wanted more for myself, but these were the people I grew up with and I wanted them to accept me—no, I *needed* them to accept me. But we could no longer relate. The things I wanted to do were considered "childish" and "nerdy." Like Shaun, I wanted to be cool. That's why I started following Darrell and his crew.

One day Darrell convinced me to go with him and his crew on one of their joyrides. There was nothing joyous about these rides; we were sneaking onto the subway trains without paying, riding up and down New York City, causing chaos. In the beginning it felt good being accepted, but I knew I wasn't cut out for this.

These so-called joyrides took place almost every weekend. As the weeks went on they got worse. We went from running through the train cars making noise to shooting spitballs at people. But things really got out of hand when Darrell decided he wanted to rob folks. I'll never forget the rumbling in my stomach when he snatched a commuter's chain off her neck and immediately ran out of the train.

I was stunned and couldn't believe this was happening. As I stood there I realized I was alone. They had all run off without me. My heart pounding, I knew the other passengers would grab me and hold me until the authorities came. My other "friends" knew he was going to do this and nobody bothered to tell me. Lucky for me, no one in the car realized I was with the group and I was spared.

Later we all met up and Darrell was laughing about the situation. I was furious; what kind of friend would leave me there like that? What if she knew I was with them? What if the cops came? I would be the one in serious trouble, and I didn't even do anything—but I was guilty by association.

You would think I'd learned my lesson after that adventure, but foolishly I didn't. I didn't want to look weak. I wanted to prove I could handle myself with the best of them, so I continued to joyride. But the next joyride changed me forever.

It was another wild weekend night with Darrell and the boys. This time we decided to terrorize the Utica Avenue station. Jumping the turnstile instead of paying our fare, we threw glass bottles on the ground, making all kinds of noises and disturbing the peace. We made our way down the long hall onto the platform waiting for the

A train. I had this terrible feeling in my stomach. A little voice inside my head was telling me to go home, but I was ignoring it.

As we made our way down to the platform, four huge men came from out of nowhere.

"Hold it right there!" they yelled.

I tried to get away, but they had us cornered. These men were undercover cops. I couldn't believe how scared I was. The first thing I thought about was my family. They would be so disappointed in me.

The cops had us up against the walls as they checked for weapons. During all this, Darrell and the boys didn't take anything serious. To this day I still can't believe how amused they were by the situation. The cops put us against the wall as bystanders watched in relief, glad the troublemakers were getting what they deserved.

What was I doing there? I wasn't a thug or troublemaker. As we were being frisked, the guys were laughing and being real jerks toward the officers. I, on the other hand, was ashamed, humiliated, and embarrassed.

For some reason the officers decided to let us go instead of taking us to the police station. They did give us a summons. But after reading it I realized the officer had purposely written the wrong information on the sheet. I believe he did it because he was trying to give us another chance.

His parting words to us were, "Don't let me see you here again."

I took the words to heart and vowed that neither he, nor any other officer, would ever have any trouble from me again.

Suddenly I realized there were signs that in the beginning I could not see, like someone was looking out for me, giving me another chance. I took that chance seriously. I caught a lot of flak from my "friends," but they had to be cut loose. It was clear to me God was letting me slide because He wanted me to do better. I stopped trying to fit in with people who were no good for me.

I told my cousin Shaun that having your own mind doesn't make you a punk. Keeping it real is not following the crowd. By the time I was a sophomore in high school, Darrell and the rest were just an afterthought. The last thing they tried to encourage me to do was attend the same high school they did. I chose one in Manhattan.

By that time I was headstrong and their teasing didn't faze me. I met a whole new set of friends who enjoyed the same things I did. Many of them are still my friends today. Making the choice to follow my heart, and God's direction, was the smartest thing I've ever done.

I lost touch with all the guys from the neighborhood. Sadly, Darrell was shot and killed during my first year of college, and the rest are in jail or on the streets. I thank God He gave me strength to love myself and be the strong-minded person I am today. I want every young person to know being different is a blessing from God—don't be ashamed of it, embrace it. If you really want to be cool, make the choice to just be yourself!

by Steven Manchester
SOMERSET, MASSACHUSETTS

After ten years of working for the Massachusetts Department of Correction, I felt the need to share the brutal experiences of prison life with those who needed to hear them most: young boys in juvenile lockup who would soon find themselves in prison if they did not start making choices toward changing their lives. As products of drugs and alcohol, domestic violence, oppressive poverty, welfare and similar systems that didn't foster healthy self-esteem, most of them could blame the world for their problems and be justified. But for the nightmare they were headed to, this attitude wasn't going to help.

My lectures always began in prayer, followed by two hours of harsh reality. I did everything I could to paint an accurate picture of life behind prison walls. Detailing rapes and murders, I tried to scare my listeners into rethinking their futures. At the same time, I did everything I could to show them they were still loved. Every session ended with applause. Yet month after month, as if they hadn't heard what I was trying to tell them, the same faces returned; they were unable to stay out of trouble. And month after month I continued speaking, hoping I might offer something that would save them from the hell I knew they faced.

After two years of volunteering my time, I seriously started to question my impact and considered quitting. Then I received a package changing my heart forever and making me choose to stay.

The night counselor at the detention center had hosted an essay contest. The assignment: *Write one to two pages explaining how Steve*

*Manchester's presentation on adult incarceration has impacted your life.*
The package contained copies of the submitted essays. Through surprised, misty eyes, I read one wonderful example after the next:

*. . . My fists were clenched tight in fear from Steve's horrific real–life stories about life in state prison. He told stories about people getting raped, killed, and [the heck] beat out of them, and it made me scared to go to prison. Steve also taught us that we still have time to turn our lives around . . .*

*. . . Steve's stories really made me think of all the stupid things I've done in my life. I hate the pain I've put on my family and friends. I'd like to thank Steve for inspiring me to change and believe in the power of hope.*

I read all twenty-six essays, and each proved another lesson in hope. I finally got to the contest winner's touching piece. It was written by a loud-mouthed twelve-year-old named Raul.

*Well, I never thought about jail like that until Steve came in. I always thought of jail totally different than what he said. I never thought that they had people with AIDS. . . . After that group I started feeling sad just thinking about what my brother must have went through. All the things that I heard from Steve [weren't] so nice. He got to my head so good that it made me think twice about life. It made me think how my future is gonna end. . . . Steve, whenever he comes back, will have my full attention again. When he first walked in I thought he was just another guy talking about things he knew nothing about. But he proved me wrong. He totally blew my mind. Everybody always told me about jail, but I didn't care. I didn't think about it like Steve made me think about it. I believed every word that came out of his mouth. He's worked there for a long time. I always told people that I'm not scared to go to jail. After this with Steve, it really had me thinking. I don't want to be someplace where I'm always watching my back, always worried about who wants to mess with me. I wouldn't make it in there. And if it comes down to a fight, you'll really be in trouble because you could get extra years in there. And me in the hole for two to three months, I'll go nuts. I don't wanna have that type of future. I have a loving family who is here for me. I got a little brother to look out for, and right now I'm not setting a good example for him. My older brother didn't set a good example for me and look what I'm doing—the same things he did. He used to call home and regret that he chilled with his boys instead of listening to my mother's advice. But now it's too late for him to change. To me I think this group is really helpful. It really made me think twice about life. I already told my mother that I would not end up like him. I don't want to call my mother someday in the future when it is too late to turn back. That's why I have to make a change in my life now that I'm young. Thanks, Steve.*

You never know when something you say or do will assist another on their U-turn journey. Raul helped me as much as he claimed I helped him. I will continue to share my stories with kids who need to hear them, thanks to Raul.

# Yes, Daddy, I Promise

by Nancy C. Anderson
HUNTINGTON BEACH, CALIFORNIA

The security guard grabbed my arm as his sharp words sliced through the air. "Come with me." He led me back inside the discount store and into the office. Then he pointed to a lime-green chair and barked, "Sit down!"

I sat.

He glared at me and said, "You can give it to me—or I can take it—your choice. What'll it be?"

I wondered, *Should I lie? . . . Should I run? . . . Should I beg? . . . Yes, begging might work.* My head dropped into my hands as I pretended to cry, "Please—can't you just let me go? I can pay you. I have money in my pocket. I'm only fourteen years old. Please, sir, I promise I'll never shoplift again." As I pulled the package of hair ribbons out of the waistband of my jeans, I could feel the sharp corner of the cardboard cutting into my stomach.

He grabbed the ribbons and said, "Save your tears, they won't work on me. I'm sick of you bratty kids stealing just for the thrill of it."

I sat up straight and pleaded, "You're not going to call my dad, are you?"

"I'm calling the police. They'll call your father."

When the officers arrived, they exchanged muffled words with the guard and the office manager. I overheard one of the policemen say, "I know her father." I also heard the phrase, "Teach her a lesson." I began to cry—real tears.

The policemen escorted me to their black-and-white car and opened the back door. As we drove through the middle of our small town, I slouched down in the seat, hoping no one could see me as I looked out the window at the evening sky. Then I saw the steeple of my family's church, and the guilt pierced me—swift and deep. *How could I have been so stupid?* I thought. *This is going to break my father's heart—and I've* already *broken God's. Oh, Lord, please forgive me.*

We arrived at the station and a round woman with a square face asked me questions until I ran out of answers. She pointed to the door of a large open cell and said, "Sit. Wait."

I walked in, and the sound of my footsteps bounced off the bars. The tears started again as I sat down on a hard bench and heard her dial the telephone. She said, "I have your daughter in a cell at the police station . . . No, she's not hurt . . . She was caught shoplifting. Can you come and get her? . . . Okay . . . You're welcome. Goodbye."

She yelled, "Hey, kid, your father's on his way."

About one hundred years later, I heard Dad's voice say my name. The woman called me up to the desk—at three times the necessary volume. I kept my eyes on the floor as I walked toward them. I saw my dad's shoes, but I didn't speak to him or look at his face, and thankfully he didn't ask me to. He signed some papers and my jailer told us, "You're free to go."

The night sky was dark and cold as we walked to the car in heavy silence. I got in and closed the door. He looked straight ahead as he drove out of the parking lot and whispered in a sad, faraway voice, "My daughter is a thief."

The five-mile drive felt like it took an hour. As we turned into our driveway, I saw my mom's silhouette at the back door. My shame bit me with jagged teeth.

After we entered the house, Dad finally spoke to me. "Let's go into the living room." Mom and Dad sat together on the couch, and I sat alone in the stiff wingback chair. He ran his fingers through his hair, looked into my eyes, and asked me, "Why?"

I told him about the first time I stole a tube of lipstick and how I felt equal amounts of thrill and guilt. Then the second time, when I took a teen magazine, the guilt faded as the thrill grew. Part of me wanted to stop the confession, but it gushed out like an open fire hydrant.

I told them about the third time, and the fourth, and the tenth.

I said, "Each time I stole, it got easier. Until now. I can see how wrong it was." Hot tears stung my face as I said, "I'm so sorry. Please forgive me—I promise never to do it again. Stealing was easy, but getting caught is hard."

Dad replied, "Yes, and it's going to get even harder." He asked Mom to bring me the notepad and pen that were sitting by the telephone. She walked over and patted my hand as she placed them in my lap. Dad continued, "Make a list of all the places you have stolen from, what you took, and how much it cost. This is your one chance for a full confession and our forgiveness. If you ever steal anything again, I will not defend you or bail you out. We will always love you, but this behavior is to stop, right here . . . right now. Do you understand?"

I looked at his face, which had suddenly aged, and said, "Yes, Daddy, I promise. No more stealing."

As I wrote my list of offenses, Mom said, "Make sure you

haven't forgotten anything; this is your only chance."

Finally I finished and said, "Here's the list." As I walked over to the couch and handed it to Dad, I asked, "What are you going to do with it?"

Dad looked at the paper and sighed. He patted the cushion and I sat down between my parents. He said, "Sometimes forgiveness is just one step on the road to full restoration. The next step, in your case, is to pay restitution—to right the wrong. So tomorrow morning we will go to all the places on your list, and you will speak to the managers. You will tell them that you have shoplifted from their stores. You will tell them exactly what you stole, apologize, and repay them. I'll loan you the money, and you'll work all summer to pay me back."

With my heart slamming and my palms sweating, I nodded.

The next morning I did exactly as he asked. It was impossibly hard, but I did it. That summer I repaid my father the money, but I will never be able to repay him for the valuable lesson he taught me about honesty and restoration. I made a choice to live an honest life. I never stole again.

# Two Cups

by Lynn Ludwick
MEDFORD, OREGON

"Hey, Mom, he's here now and we're leaving," I called down the hall to my mother in her sewing room.

"Okay. Be sure and be home by midnight," she replied.

"I will." I was seventeen and attending the local university. Since I lived at home, a curfew was still in force.

Rich helped me with my coat and we sped off in his red sports car, headed to a fraternity party. I had told my parents we were going to a dance at the student union, and they believed my lie.

The party was in full swing when we arrived. The music blared and the alcohol flowed freely. Rich was the only person I knew among his fraternity brothers, several of whom wandered down the hall with their dates. The scene was surreal, and I avoided focusing on what was going on in that apartment. I was a naïve freshman and Rich was a junior, wise in the ways of the world. We had met in French class and he had introduced me to a party life I would never have consciously chosen. But I willingly slipped into it.

He asked me what I wanted to drink. It was all new to me and I didn't know my options. "How about a Bloody Mary?" he offered, then explained what it was.

"Great. I love tomato juice."

Several drinks later I was rather wobbly, and the drive home felt like a ride on a slalom ski course. I was relieved when we pulled into my driveway.

Then reality hit me—I would have to face my father. He *always*

Choosing to Triumph

waited up until his children were safely home. *I think I'd rather jump out of an airplane without a parachute than face Dad tonight.* He was kind and reasonable, but there were strictly enforced house rules, and *No drinking!* was one of them. There was no disguising my tipsy condition.

I stumbled through the doorway and bumped into the kitchen table. *Man, Dad's going to kill me.* But the living room light was off and Dad's rhythmic snoring sang from my parents' downstairs bedroom. He was asleep!

I later lay in bed thinking how fortunate I was. If I had been caught . . . *Boy, am I lucky.*

The next morning I headed to church. My family's cross-country move a few years earlier had ended my childhood church attendance. I still believed in God, but it obviously didn't much affect my life. A month or two earlier a high school friend had invited me to her church, and on a lark, I'd accepted. The Sunday morning service was upbeat and I enjoyed the youth group. The kids were serious about their "religion," but I was there mostly for the good times. I was seventeen. Fun was my goal in life.

On that particular Sunday morning, however, my head ached as we sang "I Surrender All." *Well, not all, just some.* What if someone found out I had a hangover? I took the bread and the cup as the communion tray was passed.

"This cup is the new covenant in my blood; do this, whenever you drink it, in remembrance of me," the pastor read from 1 Corinthians 11:25.

As I held that little sip of grape juice in my hand, I sobered. I envisioned a cup of booze in my other hand. One of those cups had to go. Maybe no one else knew about the double life I was living, but God did. I had come to a fork in the road, and it was time to choose my future path. In my mind I tossed the party cup and retained the cup representing Christ's sacrificial blood. It was a beginning.

Within a few days I fully yielded my heart to God's call and accepted Christ as my Savior. As I read my Bible and evaluated my life, I came to a deeper understanding of true Christianity. I soon experienced the spiritual aspects of the youth group as well as enjoying the good times.

And I didn't date Rich anymore.

After I accepted Christ, some of the older ladies at church told me they had been praying for me and were delighted to see their prayers answered. They would never know how God had taken those prayers a step further and granted me some much needed protection.

My parents never found out about that Saturday night debacle, nor did my dad ever again go to bed before I was home for the night. It hadn't been luck at all. God certainly could have chosen to let me suffer the consequences of my behavior that night, but in His sovereignty He kindly protected me, knowing I would soon yield my heart and make a U-turn toward Him.

# Sentence Overturned!

by Carolyn Byers Ruch as told by Benjamin D. Ruch
HATFIELD, PENNSYLVANIA

My older brother can be a pain. Sometimes he seems to be on a quest to make my life miserable, picking on me from morning to night. A jab in the ribs here, a snide remark there, and I feel like a tiny mouse being tormented in the hands of a merciless giant. Yet it wasn't until I was released from an invisible prison that I realized, in spite of all of his teasing, my big brother was looking out for me. The Web history produced the evidence, three words confirmed the confession, and a swift response pronounced the conviction.

"Ben, come here, please. Your father and I need to talk to you." I could hear my mom calling to me from our home office.

This could only mean one thing—trouble. I got up from the dining room chair and walked toward the office as slowly as I could. What do they want now?

I entered the room. Three chairs were placed strategically in a circle. I knew there was no escape. I was on trial and at the mercy of my parents—the jury.

The interrogation began. "Have a seat, son." My dad instructed. Oh man, here it comes . . .

"Ben, is there anything you want to share with us?" My mom asked.

I hate that question. I mean . . . what do they want me to say? *No, I didn't take the trash out when you asked me to, and no, I didn't feed the dog today.* What do they expect me to do, willingly 'fess up to my latest violation? But I sensed this was about more than the trash and my chubby little dog missing a meal. My parents were on to something bigger. I knew it. I slouched with my eyes aimed at the floor and tried hard not to show any emotion.

"Ben, your brother checked the Web history on our new computer today and he showed your mother and me the Web address for a porn site."

He ratted on me. That jerk! I didn't look up. I kept my eyes fixed on the hardwood floor at my feet.

"Ben, do you know anything about this?" my mom added.

I wanted a way out. I knew there wasn't any. My parents would never give up until they had answers. I knew this from experience. When the two of them find evidence, they won't stop until they crack the case. I decided to come clean. Sweat began to ooze from my pores. They'll never understand. I struggled for words to express my secret shame, as each moment of quietness ticked slowly by.

"It was me." I sighed. I glanced up quickly and saw my mom's face. She was fighting tears. I could tell. She knows how much I hate it when she cries. My eyes darted to the floor. I felt sick. The silence continued. I waited for a verdict. My parents didn't know I was already a prisoner—a prisoner involved in a secret war. This wasn't the first time I'd seen porn. Man, they're going to freak when I tell them this. Breaking the silence, I began to talk.

"I was playing with some friends back in the field and we decided to check out the Hangout." (A crude fort constructed with a few boards nailed to some trees—it was a local teenager hangout in my neighborhood.) I went on to explain that was where I found a pornographic magazine. "When I first picked it up, I didn't realize what it was. The front cover was ripped off, no doubt to disguise it, and the first few pages had furniture on them. Then I flipped to the next page."

I remember it like it was yesterday. I stared at the page. My mind and body were at war. My mind warned, *No, this is wrong. Don't look!* My body screamed, *Look! This is what you're made for—this is what life's about.*

Suddenly I realized this was the kind of magazine my parents had warned me about, so I decided to destroy it, ripping it into shreds—feeding my curiosity . . . page by toxic page.

"It's like those pictures got stuck in the back of my head," I mumbled. No matter how hard I tried to forget them, I couldn't. It was as if they came to life, constantly teasing and tormenting me until I gave in to temptation. I continued. "One day you left to run an errand, Mom, so I looked for a Web site."

It's funny, the longer I talked the better I felt. I could sense a bizarre feeling of relief. My secret was out. Yet I was still sweating it. I had no idea what my parents would do as I sat waiting for their next line of questioning. The questions never came. Oddly enough, my parents understood.

"Your dad and I understand temptation and failure, Ben. We are well acquainted with our own sins. We both struggle each and every day to make wise and holy choices. That's why we need Jesus in our lives. You're not alone. We want to help you win this battle."

"Ben, you've entered a war zone," my dad warned with the intensity of a decorated war veteran who never left the battlefield—a fellow soldier continuing to stand guard to protect himself and his troops each and every day.

"Pornography will seek to destroy you and everyone you love

now and in the future. Your mother and I have seen marriages torn apart by its addictive power; however, we want you to know we are here to fight this beast with you. We will do whatever it takes to help you destroy this enemy that seeks to control your mind."

Within days my parents installed a filtering system on our new computer, and they vowed to never again plug in a computer at our house without first having a filtration system lined up and ready to go. I was relieved by the limits they set on my computer time. I didn't want the pressure of the temptation.

But it was a choice I made on my own that became my best weapon in fighting the monster called porn. Entering the kitchen one morning, I announced, "Mom, I have a new password to get on the computer." My mom turned to look at me, eyebrows raised, with a look of intrigue.

"Oh yeah? What is it?" she asked.

"WWJDIMP."

"WWJDIMP." She repeated. "Well, I know what WWJD means, but what does the IMP mean?"

"What Would Jesus Do In My Position," I stated confidently. My mom smiled. I had made a choice to divide and conquer with the most valuable weapon in my arsenal—Jesus! Yes, porn would always be there to tempt and entice me, but with Jesus as my defender—sentence overturned!

# Journal to a Friend

by Carol Oyanagi

MINNEAPOLIS, MINNESOTA

June 30:

*I wish everyone would let me run my own life! No one cares what I think. I do my homework, get good grades, and make my parents and teachers proud of me. People take advantage of me. They push me around. Tell me what to do. Tell me how to live. And I take it, like I always have. Well, look at the mess my life has been! I try to tell people how I feel, and they just find some way to make me feel terrible. Always. I can't help the way I am. But in my future I'm going to make it big and accomplish great things so I can show this world what I'm made of!*

These are the typical journal entries I wrote as a young girl of only fifteen years old. Everyone thought I was a shy, sweet person. That's what they saw on the outside. On the inside I was angry, confused, and full of rage. I felt I had no control over my life.

I started my journal-writing habit in seventh grade. Right before going to sleep, I sat with my knees hunched up under my bedcovers and wrote about what had happened during the day. Now that I am in high school, things have become more complicated. As the pressures of life have increased, I find myself writing longer entries. Many times I can't wait to get home so I can explode all my thoughts into the pages of my palm-sized tablet. Sometimes I write two entries a day.

I've never shared my feelings with my parents or siblings because I don't want them to get upset. I'm also afraid they'll say I shouldn't have such feelings. I can't tell my friends, either. Initially they'll sympathize with me, but later they'll make fun of how sensitive I am or tell my secret fears to others. Journal writing has become my only source of expression. I hide my writing so no one will know I have such negative feelings about life.

I don't really know who I am talking to as I commit my feelings to paper. Maybe myself? An imaginary friend? It's taken a few years and several journals to realize it is God.

Often I pause in the middle of writing my feelings. Then as I finish an entry, I write positive words. My paragraphs form into comforting statements about myself or other people. An inexplicable understanding flows from my mind through my pen and down onto the paper. I discover ways to solve issues or respond to someone who said something nasty to me. God is listening to me. He is helping me.

Often I find I can't keep up with the stress, complex relationships, and emotional turmoil I face each day. Since I somehow know God is speaking to me through my writing, I've started talking back to Him. And does He get an earful!

"Why me?" I ask. "God, why did you make me this way, so sensitive, so unsure of myself? I don't understand."

Sometimes there is a pause. Then I calm down as God's answer flows through my writing: "I'm different for a reason," or "I just need to wait a little longer," or "God has a purpose for me." I don't always get an immediate response. I am impatient at times, and I don't wait long enough; at other times there is only silence.

Gradually I've started asking God for things directly, writing them down, and praying for other people. Later, as I read those entries, I begin to notice a pattern. God put the puzzle pieces of my life into place, making them fit together in the bigger picture. At first I didn't understand everything, but I realize I don't have to figure it all out, because my journals prove God is in control of my life. Maybe I don't get the answer I expect, but I still get an answer. Sometimes God even answers my prayers before I write them down. I don't have to wait until I am home, alone with my journal, before talking to Him and allowing Him to comfort me. Instead of seeing God as another authority figure, trying to tell me how to run my life, I see Him as my best friend. He gives me answers, lets me fail, and yet still loves me. And sometimes I don't even mind letting Him take over once in a while.

# choosing salvation

*Then my soul will rejoice in the Lord and delight in his salvation. My whole being will exclaim, "Who is like you, O Lord?"* —Psalm 35:9–10a

There's an old joke about a guy who knew a flood was coming, so he asked God to save him. First a rescue squad came by, but he said, "No thanks, God will save me." Then a boat came by, but he still refused their help. When the waters were too high, he climbed on his rooftop and a helicopter came, but he waved them off, preferring to wait for God. Finally he drowned and went to heaven where he asked God, "Why didn't you save me?" God responded, "I sent you the rescue squad, the boat, and the helicopter. What more did you want?" Are we waiting for that white knight to come racing in to fight our battles? Listen up; God already sent us a Savior. His name is Jesus and He died for our sins, paid our debt, and conquered death. All for us. Now, we can sit on our proverbial rooftop or let Him lift us from what keeps us in the flood of guilt and shame. Choose salvation. It's not cheap, but it is all paid for and free.

# Fifteen Months

by Christy Heitger-Casbon as told by Jason Gomez
NOBELSVILLE, INDIANA

Only five minutes left of my last high school youth group. I had been with these same loving, Christian people most of my life. The thought of drugs or stealing or living with strangers would never have even entered my mind. Instead, tears stung my eyes as I remembered retreats, church lock-ins, pizza parties, and progressive dinners. As we bowed our heads and grasped hands for the closing prayer, I found myself tightening my grip, both physically and emotionally. I did not know how to let go.

Everyone was excited as they said good-bye. Everyone was heading off to different colleges. Everyone but me. I was staying in my hometown to attend Florida State University. I wasn't moving anywhere, not even out of my parents' house. Everyone left. The room was empty as I stood there frozen, feeling alone, afraid, and abandoned.

That fall, with no friends, no girlfriend, not even a college roommate, I felt lonely and depressed. I started hanging out with Rick and Brian, two guys I had known since middle school, but not from youth group. They were not the kind of people I would have hung out with in high school, but they were familiar faces who were stuck at home like me.

I had a serious case of the blues when Rick suggested, "Pot will chase your blues away." With that statement, he pulled out some marijuana and lit a joint.

My eyes widened. "Nn-nn-noooo, thanks," I stammered nervously. As the smell of marijuana permeated the room, I grew tense.

"We're hitting a club tonight," Brian said. "Come with us."

"Yeah, come on," Rick urged.

I thought about saying no, but I was afraid they might ditch me for good.

"You'll have fun," Brian promised.

I was old enough to go and do whatever I wanted. It was not like they were asking me to drink or do drugs. They just wanted me to go with them. I would just go to hang out and maybe meet some new people.

For the next month, I went to a bunch of parties. The drill always seemed the same. People offered me drugs, I declined, and then they'd look at me funny. Some even asked why I came if I wasn't getting high. After a while I started asking myself the same question. Maybe I should say yes just once. I had not seen anything bad happen to anyone. It seemed safe enough; no one was vomiting, blacking out, or being carried out on a stretcher.

One night I sat down next to a beautiful girl with long red hair and deep green eyes. She offered me her joint.

"One time won't hurt you," she said.

I caved. I reached for the joint, placed it between my lips, and inhaled. As I sucked in, guilt enveloped me. This isn't right, I thought. I should stop. In an instant, the drug took hold, the guilt faded, and as I scanned the room, I suddenly had a new perspective. I wasn't the outcast anymore. Rick was right; pot was chasing my blues away. For the first time in a long while, I was happy, relaxed, and accepted.

After that, it became increasingly easier to give in to temptation. Within weeks, I was smoking pot daily. Since I lived at home, my parents could tell I was doing drugs. They begged me to stop and I refused, so they adopted the "tough love" mentality and kicked me out.

A sober friend felt sorry for me and let me move in with him, but because I spent all my money on drugs, I couldn't afford rent. He soon booted me out, too. I quickly learned the fine art of mooching and began hopping from place to place, crashing on different people's floors. Most of those people were junkies who exposed me to more drugs, including acid (LSD), cocaine, crack, crystal meth, heroin, and Ecstasy.

Although I didn't have any living expenses, I was still broke and desperate for drugs. One Friday night I asked a dealer what I could trade for cocaine.

"I like your pants," he told me. "Hand 'em over and I'll set you up."

Without hesitation, I stripped down to my underwear and gave him my pants. Broke and homeless, my pride vanished along with my morals.

Without so much as a glimmer of guilt, I began stealing from the fast-food restaurant where I worked in order to support my addiction. Stealing enabled me to party more and experiment with new drugs.

One night I tried magic mushrooms. Soon my carefree mind went numb, and I began hallucinating. My paranoid eyes darted around the room as I watched my friends with heightened suspicion. I was sure they were trying to kill me. Dizziness overwhelmed me. I couldn't tell up from down. As sweat rolled down my forehead, I glanced at my chest and saw my heart pounding hard and fast through my shirt. Am I dying, I wondered? Freaked out and scared to death, I pleaded with a friend to take me to my parents' house.

When Mom opened the door, her face turned white. "What's wrong with you?" she gasped.

Hysterically I repeated over and over that I was insane and dying. Mom frantically called 9-1-1. The paramedics and police arrived to a chaotic scene. My younger brother and sister watched in horror as the police handcuffed me, put me in the ambulance, and rushed me to the hospital.

There, doctors pumped my stomach to empty the drugs from my system. My near-death experience scared me enough to abandon drugs for a few weeks. That was as long as I could resist, afraid or not. With no drug parties and no drug friends, I was miserable and lonely again. Fear alone did not keep me company or give me a life. In fact, I wanted to get rid of the fear.

A short time passed before I was back at it again. I arrived at a party and immediately felt at home. The music was pumping so loud my chest vibrated. The smoke was so thick my eyes burned.

"Here, have some Ecstasy," a girl offered.

I considered saying no, but I couldn't resist. Before long, I was flying. Why did I ever stop, I wondered. This is awesome! Then a shriek from the bathroom shattered my hypnotic state. I rushed to see what was wrong.

"They won't move!" a girl cried, referring to two guys lying on the floor motionless, staring into space.

I kneeled down and studied their hollow, lifeless eyes—eyes that didn't even blink.

"What are they on?" I asked a guy who'd been partying with them.

"Ecstasy," he said, "They must've gotten a bad batch."

Shivers shot through my spine. I was high on Ecstasy. Will I end up in a coma, too? Or worse? I panicked. I knew then things had to change. If I survive this, I promised myself, I'm gonna stop. I left the party and crashed at a junkie's trashed apartment. I sat down in the kitchen, cradled my head in my hands, and stared down at the filthy floor. The vision of those guys' lifeless eyes haunted me. That could've been me! Why has this happened to me?

Then I realized this hadn't happened to me. I did it to myself. I was at this dead end because I'd cut God out of my life. It was a profound, yet simple, revelation. I fell to my knees sobbing. "Please forgive me, Lord! I've been sinning, and I'm sorry. Help me!" I pleaded. For hours, I continued pouring out my heart to Him. Then, drawing from His strength, I picked up the phone, called my parents, and asked for help.

Mom had a friend who told her about a Bible-based organization called Teen Challenge located in West Virginia. Through a yearlong residential program, they help adolescents deal with life-controlling problems and focus on total rehabilitation.

When we arrived at the center, I felt rattled. I wondered if I'd survive rehab. Jim, the director of the program, approached me.

"Don't be nervous," he said. "I'm here to help, not judge you."

I looked closely at Jim's sincere eyes and felt safe. I knew the road ahead would be hard, but his warm reassurance told me I wouldn't walk it alone. I knew I was making the most important U-turn of my life. As part of this new group, one by one, we united in Christ. I grew close with other residents as we confessed our sins and discussed our addictions. Over the next few months, their support helped me move toward freedom.

One day at group, Jim asked me, "How have you changed since you stopped doing drugs?"

"When I was using, my heart was empty and bitter," I explained. "But now I'm filled with Christ's love."

"What's that like?" Jim asked.

"It's like for fifteen months, I stopped breathing," I said. "But when I chose to turn to Jesus, He brought me back to life."

Choosing Salvation

# Fire on the Mountain Tonight

by Laura L. Smith
OXFORD, OHIO

"What are you going to wear tonight?" Tami asked as she removed her silver bracelets.

I pulled the ponytail holder out of my matted hair and waited to hear Lauren's response. I had stuffed a pair of cutoff shorts and a lavender tank top with a satin ribbon trim into my duffel bag, but I also packed a plain white T-shirt. I was debating over which top to wear to the big campfire. I wanted to look cute since this was our last night at camp, but I didn't want to look too put together for a fire on the mountainside.

"I'm just wearing my Marmon Valley T-shirt with khaki shorts," Lauren called from the shower. "It's too hot to think about an outfit."

"I think I'll wear something black," Tami laughed. Lauren and I giggled with her. Tami wore something black every day.

"T-shirt and shorts for me," I gurgled while immersing my head in the cold jets of water. I'll just be casual, I decided. This night was about more than looks.

After dinner, it was time to hike up the slope to the week's finale, the campfire on the mountain. The older campers and their counselors would make the climb up the hillside. This was our first year as senior campers and our first time to be included in the bonfire ritual. Lauren stood in the middle, with Tami and me on each side of her, arm in arm, singing songs and giggling as we made our ascent.

I could smell the rich smoke of the fire before I could see it.

Several campers had already staked out seats on the large logs that served as benches angling around the bonfire. We walked toward the roaring orange and red flames. The heat and smoke brought tears to the corners of my eyes. Counselors were doling out marshmallows to roast. After cooking and eating our sticky treats, Lauren, Tami, and I settled into seats halfway back from the blaze.

By now, most everyone was here. The counselors stood up, one at a time, and told memorable stories from the week. As we clapped and stomped in applause, the guitars started playing.

Music was always my favorite part of each camp day. Although my singing voice was as melodious as a sea gull's, I loved to belt out the rhythmic tunes. We sang at the end of every meal, and since Marmon Valley was a Christian camp, we sang Christian songs. I had never known praising God could be so much fun. All of the songs at my pristine church were played on the organ, and the hymnal dated most of them as being written in the 1800s.

The counselors led us in some of our favorites. They sang the verses, and we shouted back the choruses. Then the mood changed. The strumming got softer. What was this next song? I couldn't tell which one it was, yet I was sure I had heard it before.

The smoke from the fire seemed whiter, or was it just easier to see it now against the darkening sky? When had the sun gone down? When had the stars come out to light up the evening? I reached out my arms and placed them on Tami's and Lauren's shoulders. Automatically, they put their arms around me, too. We swayed to the soft melody.

No one was singing, yet the guitars kept playing this beautiful tune. Then Steve, one of the counselors, stood up. Tami, Lauren, and I all had professed serious crushes on Steve the first night in our bunks. He was cute and funny.

"I am a Christian," Steve said. "Four years ago on this very night I dedicated my life to Jesus Christ, and my life has never been the same. We hope your week here has been fun. We hope you have learned a lot about horsemanship and made a lot of friends, but we hope you have experienced something more. We hope you have gotten to know our Lord."

Goose bumps crept up my arms and legs. What was he saying? It felt as if he were speaking directly to me.

The other counselors joined Steve. They all stood in front of us, arm in arm. The music continued and they began singing softly,

*"There's a fire on the mountain tonight,*
*Nowhere to run, nowhere to hide . . ."*

We sang this song all week, but differently on this night. We usually sang it loudly and quickly with upbeat verses, strategic hand-claps, and foot stomps. I had never paused to consider what the lyrics meant. Steve continued over the soft singing, "I invite any of you here who feel called to choose Jesus as your personal Savior to come forward at this time." Something tugged at me.

Was anybody really going to go up? Should I go? What did it mean to invite Jesus into your heart? I was already a Christian, wasn't I? I went to church almost every Sunday with my parents. I could never get up in front of this whole group. Were Tami and Lauren going to go up? What would they think if I walked forward . . . or if I didn't?

As if pulled by a magnet, my body stood up without weighing the consequences of its actions. I struggled to sit down before I embarrassed myself, yet my feet moved forward. Cecilia, my riding instructor, reached out as I approached the front. She ushered me to a smooth spot on the ground where we could sit. The heat of the fire distorted my vision. Everything looked wavy and out of focus.

"Laura," Cecilia said in a near-whisper to me, "do you take Jesus as your personal Savior?"

"I do," the words came out of my mouth. I was completely unprepared for the emotions that swept over me. My entire body was emptied. My whole self left the thirteen-year-old girl's frame wearing the cut-off shorts and white T-shirt. I felt a chill and an empty aching as I gasped for air. Then, as quickly as my old being had been drained, a new self filled me. I felt warm and tingly. Tears poured down my face as all of the fear, shame, and uncertainty I ever felt was replaced by a pure and beautiful love like I had never experienced.

Cecilia held me and we rocked. I don't know how long we sat like that. I lost all sense of time and space. From the moment I knelt on the ground with Cecilia to the time she stood me up was a blur. When had the music stopped? When had the fire burned down to embers? Had anyone else come forward? What had the campers who had remained in their seats done? I didn't have the answers, but it didn't matter. None of it mattered. I was different. God lived within me. The Holy Spirit had come to live in me. With God's love, I could do anything. The things I wanted to do were different, too. I couldn't wait to share my experience with my friends, my family, and my world.

My senses somewhat revived, I glanced around for Lauren and Tami. I didn't see Lauren, but Tami was walking toward me. I could tell she had prayed the same prayer I had. Her eyes were glowing with His incomparable love.

"Let's go," she whispered.

We made our way toward the mulch path. Tami's arm felt just right around my waist. As we started our descent, we sang together the rest of the chorus.

*"Tell me, would you be okay, if you had to die today?*
*There's a fire on the mountain tonight."*

# High on Jesus

by Mary Lee Brown as told by Dave

SEQUIM, WASHINGTON

I was hungry, I couldn't remember the last time I'd eaten. Maybe it was a couple of days before. A friend and I finished practicing our guitars, scarfed down some hamburgers and the last of the chips just as my mom got home from work.

"I'm not buying any more groceries," she raged. "From now on, your sister and I will eat out."

Tearfully she added I could starve for all she cared, I needed to show some initiative and either go back to school or get a job. She wasn't kidding! Since I was high on dope, I only smiled while she ranted and raved. After all, I had a full belly. I really didn't care about her, my sister, or myself.

Now I was wishing for a burger or a bag of chips. My hunger had me walking down Seventh Avenue, trying to remember what the guy in the park last week had said about free meals. I hadn't paid much attention to him because I was high then, not hungry. Now I needed that address. I'd opened the last can of beans from my meager shopping trip, which took the last dollar in my pocket. I had to find the place with the free meals. The empty pantry at my house reminded me Mom wasn't going to relent. She was still angry. I was only sixteen, which meant my mom was legally responsible for me, but she wasn't going to feed me unless I changed my ways.

I'd walked a couple of miles before I realized I had no idea where I was. I was getting hungrier by the minute. This was an unfamiliar part of the city. The streets were deserted. After looking at the dilapidated buildings, I understood why there wasn't anyone walking on

Choosing Salvation

the sidewalks. Just me. It was spooky.

I became aware of someone walking behind me. I glanced back. A raggedy-looking man was about twenty yards behind me. I walked faster. If he was going to rob me, he wasn't going to get much, but I didn't want any trouble.

"Son, wait up," he called.

I stopped, figuring I could overpower him if he tried anything.

"The place you're looking for is three blocks over there," he said as he walked up to me. He pointed to the left of where I stood. I was so relieved at his friendly tone, I mumbled "Thanks," and took off in the direction he pointed. Sure enough, there was a building with a line of people standing outside waiting to go in. The sign on the building said *Friendship Chapel*. Not exactly what I had in mind. I wanted food. Not sermons.

I approached a shabby old man standing in line and asked, "Do you know if they serve food around here?"

"Sure, but first you go to chapel. Then you eat. Get in line."

I got in line behind him and an assortment of about twenty unkempt, sad-looking men and women a lot older than me. The strong smell of unwashed bodies made me wonder if I was hungry enough to eat in the same room as this motley group.

I'm here, I might as well, I thought, but this is stupid. Why should I have to listen to some old preacher in order to get food? I filed in with the others and took a back seat in the small stuffy room. I hoped this wasn't going to last very long. With all the foul smells, it wouldn't take long for the stink to be overwhelming. It was a plain room with a few rows of wooden benches and a small table in front. It didn't look like any church I'd ever been in. What I didn't expect to see was the guy standing in front of the table, waiting for everyone to sit down. He caught my eye and smiled.

I couldn't believe my eyes. It was the guy in the park who told me about this place and the free food. He hadn't mentioned the chapel service. The conversation in the park came back to me. He was saying the same things to this group of people . . . hungry people . . . waiting to be fed. I caught the phrase "bread of life," but I was only half listening. He continued with, "The blood of Jesus has washed away all your sins." That's what he'd said in the park! It hadn't made any sense then; I was stoned. I listened more closely now. Tears filled my eyes.

Someone really did care! This stranger cared. He told us that Jesus loved us all and had died on the cross for us so our sins could be forgiven. A few minutes later he invited us to come forward if we wanted to know Jesus. I gripped the wooden seat, unwilling to make a fool out of myself, but I felt as though I was propelled out of my seat. I found myself walking down the aisle to the front of the room, unaware of anything but this man standing there with his hand out to me. Tears flowed down my face. He took my hand and we knelt together on the hard floor. He prayed the simple prayer of salvation with me. I sobbed, ashamed of the way I had acted the past year and the way I had treated my mom and my sister.

As this man knelt there with his arm around my shoulder, all the loneliness, fear, and hurt drained out of me. I hadn't even known how deep those feelings were. A great weight lifted from me, and I felt light as air. This time it wasn't dope making me high. It was Jesus.

Later, as my new friend and I ate our simple meal together in the dining hall, he told me that ever since he met me in the park, he'd prayed for me. When I told him about trying to find this place and about the man coming up behind me to give me directions, I suddenly realized that man had no way of knowing where I was headed! Where had he gone? He left as suddenly as he appeared, as if out of nowhere. My friend smiled and said, "I would venture to say that he was your guardian angel. We all have one, you know. You were given a special blessing by getting to meet yours!"

My life changed that night. I never felt a need to smoke dope again. The man, Pastor Billy, and I became close friends. Every Sunday he took me to his church. On Wednesday nights, a few people would get together to play music and talk about the Lord.

My mother's life also began to change that night. I started praying for my mom. A few weeks later, she, too, came to know Jesus. I demonstrated to my mom and my sister that I was serious about the U-turn I had made toward God. I got a job and I have made a plan to go back to school. This isn't a joke, it's how it happened.

As a result of my choice, we are a family once again—my mom, sister, Jesus, and me. And I don't ever plan to go hungry again, physically or spiritually.

# Dating God

by Christy Carlson
ORANGE PARK, FLORIDA

Like most seventeen-year-old girls, I was hoping for my knight in shining armor to walk up and sweep me off my feet. I had dated a few friends, and even managed to meet a couple of nice guys around town. But none of them was exactly right for me. All my friends had great boyfriends, so why couldn't I seem to find one?

I dated a guy pretty seriously when I was sixteen, and was devastated when he broke off the relationship. I was so sure he was to be my high school sweetheart. I wanted someone who would call me each night and ask me how my day went. I wanted a boyfriend to take me on dates and to dances. After that relationship ended, I tired of searching for a decent guy.

On Thursday nights my friends and I gathered at the local skating rink. That's where I met Joey, a floor guard. His job was to skate around the rink and make sure no one was going too fast or breaking any rules. I first noticed him when he called to me across the floor.

"Hey, I like your shirt!"

I was wearing a shirt emblazoned with Larry the Cucumber from *Veggie Tales*. I glanced over and thanked him, noticing his incredibly good looks. He was tall with short blond hair and chiseled features. In other words, he was drop-dead gorgeous.

Joey skated over to me and introduced himself. We skated side by side for the rest of the evening. He made me laugh by doing voice imitations and complimented me on everything from my shirt to my personality. I left the rink that night looking forward to seeing him again next Thursday.

Joey and I got to know each other pretty well over the next few weeks. I was head over heels for him. Yet I knew he wasn't the type of guy I could bring home to my parents. Joey was twenty-three years old, six years older than I was. I learned that Joey liked to party and drink alcohol. I figured he had also been with his share of women.

My Christian parents would never go for him. I dated only guys who attended church and shared the same beliefs as I did. It was out of character for me to fall for a guy like Joey. But I was lonely, Joey was good-looking, and I loved how he shamelessly flirted with me.

In the back of my mind I could hear the Holy Spirit warn, "Christy, he's wrong for you. Do not be unequally yoked with non-believers."

I pushed those thoughts from my head, ignoring what I knew was true. I was enjoying myself too much to be discouraged.

For a few months, things were going great. Although not officially dating, we would see each other at the rink, talk on the phone, and send each other notes. I found myself at the rink several times a week instead of only on Thursdays. I loved being around Joey.

One night I decided to surprise him and showed up at the rink on a night I usually didn't go there. I walked in and saw him skating beside another girl. He was talking to her and she was laughing. He casually put his arm around her.

I could feel my heart beating against my ribs. I suddenly realized I never really meant anything to him. In the blink of an eye it became crystal clear: I was just someone else for Joey to flirt with. Embarrassed and angry with myself, I realized God was right. Why didn't I listen to Him? I knew He always had my best interests at heart. I let my loneliness get between God and me.

That night I made a promise to God and chose to take a U-turn in my life. I got down on my knees in my bedroom and rededicated my life to Him. Instead of searching out a boyfriend, I put my complete trust in God. I would "date" God until He brought someone into my life that was right for me. I wouldn't think about having a boyfriend until the Lord allowed one to enter my life.

Two weeks later I met Jonathan. I was not looking for a boyfriend, but the Lord placed him right in front of me. He was everything I was looking for in a guy. He was a strong Christian and shared my beliefs and morals. He made me laugh. He treated me like a lady.

Jonathan turned out to be my knight in shining armor. He swept me off my feet. I never would have found him without the Lord's help.

When we think we know what's best for ourselves, we must remember God always knows what's better. And if we stray (or in my case, skate) from God's will, we must also remember we can always choose to make a U-turn and get right back on track.

# And a Teen Will Lead Him

by Nancy B. Gibbs
CORDELE, GEORGIA

Daddy was incoherent, unaware of his surroundings or my presence. His ability to speak almost gone and unable to move, he was at the mercy of everyone around him. He could no longer feed himself or even reach for a glass of water. I knew we were sharing the precious last few days of his life. The room was frightfully quiet. The only sound in the room was Dad's rattled, labored breathing.

"Please let him go on to heaven now," I whispered, breaking the silence in the room. My tears fell on the pillow of the man I had loved for my entire life. As I prayed, I felt the nudging of the Holy Spirit who brought to mind a sweet memory. It was the memory of the day I heard Jesus knock on the door of my heart. It was the day that Dad and I let Jesus into our lives.

When I was growing up, Sunday mornings didn't involve going to church. My mother occasionally spoke about God and His love for us. I picked up the basics about how God created the earth and wanted us to do good things. I didn't know or understand the Bible stories that fascinated so many kids. I wasn't familiar with the church songs many of my peers had memorized. At age ten, however, I knew deep in my heart that one day I would serve God in a powerful way. When I look back, I wonder how I knew. There were no Bible verses and few sermons to guide me. But I whispered to God many times as I was growing up. I told Him that when I became a woman, I would give my life to Him.

As I grew from a child to a teen, my life took a drastic change. I withdrew from my family. My grades were passing, but low. No matter what I did, I was average. I did not like being average. I did not like "me" much at all. Life seemed empty, lonely, and sad.

When I was seventeen, I attended a church service. It was a big room filled with people singing and praising Jesus. I thought it was a wonderful place. I found myself wishing my family could have come with me.

The pastor talked about a loving God. I was amazed when he said God loved all people. Did that include me—the quiet girl who was just average? How could He love me? I didn't even love me.

I felt a strange sensation in my heart. I had never felt anything like it before. I knew Jesus was knocking on the door of my heart that morning. I didn't understand much about spiritual things, but I understood at that very moment, God was asking me to give my life to Him.

"I'll ask Mom and Daddy to come with me tonight, God," I whispered. "I'll give my life to you then." The pastor asked the congregation to put down the hymnbooks and bow our heads in prayer. I was so relieved. Then suddenly when I closed my eyes and began praying, I started trembling. Tears flowed from my eyes. As I looked up, the pastor was standing directly in front of me.

*How did he know?* I wondered. He reached out to take my hand and I could not resist the urge to accept Christ any longer. I ran to the altar alone. I made a confession of faith and accepted the gift of salvation. My baptism was scheduled for that evening. I couldn't wait to get home to tell my parents what happened that morning.

"We all have to go to church tonight," I shouted when I walked in the back door. "I'm going to be baptized." I told them about how I felt Jesus calling my name and the way I responded.

That evening, as a family, we arrived at church early. The baptism was to follow the sermon. To my surprise, my father and brother went down to the altar and accepted Christ as their Savior, too. We were baptized together.

Years later I recalled that U-turn journey as my dad stirred in his bed and I reached out and took his hand. He squeezed it gently when I began to pray aloud.

"Yes," my heart told me. "Daddy is headed for heaven." His trip began on a Sunday morning more than twenty years earlier, when I was a teen. I went to church and answered yes to Jesus when He knocked on the door of my heart. As soon as I let Jesus in, He brought my dad in, too. The choices we make not only change our lives but those around us, as well. What an awesome wonder is God's love for us all.

# The Day the Cheering Stopped

by Gloria Cassity Stargel as told by John C. Stewart

GAINESVILLE, GEORGIA

It happened on a cold day in January, midway through my senior year in high school. I tossed my books into the locker and reached for my black-and-gold Cougar jacket. From down the corridor, a friend called out, "Good luck, Johnny. I hope you get the school you want."

Playing football was more than a game for me. It was my *life*. So the world looked wonderful as I headed up the hill toward the gym to learn which college wanted me on its team.

How I counted on the resulting scholarship—had for years! It held my only hope for higher education. My dad, an alcoholic, left home long ago and Mom worked two jobs to keep seven children fed. I held part-time jobs to help out.

I wasn't worried. I had the grades I needed. Ever since grammar school, I lived and breathed football. It was my identity. Growing up in a little southern town where football is king, my skills on the field made me a big man in the community as well as on campus. I pictured myself on that pedestal.

Everyone around me pumped my ego. The local newspaper wrote about me; at football games, exuberant cheerleaders yelled out my name. People said things like, "You can do it, Johnny. You can go all the way to professional football!" That was heady stuff and I ate it up. It kind of made up for not having a dad to encourage me along the way.

Hurrying to the gym, I recalled all those football games—and all those *injuries*! I never let any of them slow me down for long, not

Choosing Salvation

the broken back or the messed-up shoulders and knees. I just gritted my teeth and played through the agony. I *had* to.

Now the reward came. A good future would be worth the price I paid. So with a confident grin on my face, I sprinted into Coach Stone's office.

Coach sat behind his desk, the papers from my file spread before him. Our three other coaches sat around the room. No doubt about it, this lineup signaled a momentous occasion.

"Have a seat, Johnny." Coach motioned to the chair beside his desk. "Johnny," he started, "you've worked really hard. You've done a good job for us. Several colleges want to make you an offer."

Something about his tone made me nervous. I shifted my sitting position.

"But Johnny," he said, holding my medical records in his hands, "Doctor Kendley can't recommend you for college football. One more bad hit and you could be paralyzed for life. We can't risk it."

A long silence followed. Then Coach Stone's eyes met mine. "I'm sorry, Johnny. There will be no scholarship."

*No scholarship?* The blow hit me like a three-hundred-pound linebacker slamming against my chest. Somehow I got out of that office. I could not believe they were only thinking of my welfare. Instead, in my mind, a punching bag reverberated. *You're not good enough, you're not good enough, you're not good enough.*

*Suddenly the cheering stopped. Without the cheering, I was nothing. And without college, I would stay* a nothing.

After that I gave up. In so doing, I lost my moorings. At first I settled for beer and marijuana. Soon I got into the hard stuff: acid, PCP, heroin, cocaine. I tried them all. When graduation rolled around, I wondered how I made it through the ceremonies.

Several older friends tried to talk to me about God. Yet even though I had grown up in church and had served as an altar boy, I couldn't grasp the fact that God had anything to do with my present problems.

I decided to hit the road with a couple of buddies. We had no money and no goal. Along the way we stole gas to keep us going. When we got hungry enough, we picked up odd jobs. No matter how little food we had, we always managed to get more drugs.

My anger continued to fester. It wasn't long until I got into a fight and landed in jail thousands of miles from home. It caused me to take a good look at myself and see how low I had sunk. This began my choice to make a slow U-turn back to God.

"God," I prayed for the first time in years, "please help me. I'm lost and I can't find my way back."

I didn't hear an immediate answer, and I didn't clean up my act. My friends and I *did* head toward home, but the old car quit on us.

I went to a garage, hoping to get some cheap parts. *Maybe I can patch 'er up enough to get us home.* I was tired, hungry, dirty—and very much under the influence. Yet a man extended a hand of friendship. He even took us to supper.

After we were fed, Mr. Brown called me aside. "Son," he said, "you don't have to live like this. You can be somebody if only you'll try. God will help you. Remember, He loves you, and so do I."

I was buffaloed. He seemed to care about me. He called me son. It had been a long, long time since a man had called me son.

That night, in my sleeping bag, I gazed up at the star-filled Texas night. The sky looked so close, I thought I could reach up and

Choosing Salvation

touch it. Once again I tried to pray. "Lord, I am *so* tired. If you'll have me, I'm ready to come back to you."

In my heart, I heard Him answer, "I'm here. Come on back, son. I'm here." He called me son, just like Mr. Brown did! I liked that.

On the road again, I thought, *If Mr. Brown, a complete stranger, thinks I can make something of myself, maybe I can.*

I didn't straighten out all at once. But I started trying, and God kept sending people to help me. Like Susan. In September, this cute, casual friend from high school came up to me at a football game, of all places. She kissed me on the cheek. "Welcome home, Johnny."

I quit using drugs permanently the day she told me, "Johnny, if you keep doing drugs, I can't date you anymore."

I still can feel the sting of that day—the day the cheering stopped. The hurt doesn't linger, though. Once I chose to make my U-turn and it was complete, I learned I could live without the cheers. After all, I have a caring heavenly Father who calls me son.

This reminds me. I *do* have a cheering section—a heavenly one. Check out this Bible verse I discovered: "There is rejoicing in the presence of the angels of God over one sinner who repents" (Luke 15:10).

How about that? Angels! Cheering for *me*! I like that.

# He Lives With Me, But We're Not Married—and Mom Approves!

by Michele D. Newhouse

EDMOND, OKLAHOMA

Before I met Christ, I knew Him as I might have known the president—I knew a lot of facts about Him, I respected Him, and I knew He impacted people's lives in a very real way. But it wasn't until I was thirteen years old that I actually *met* Jesus and learned the difference between knowing *about* Him and *getting to know* Him personally. I was at a Christian summer camp, and the speaker used an analogy that really spoke to my heart.

I was attending camp in the piney woods of east Texas. Pine Cove is a marvelous non-denominational camp, and my experience was a total delight in so many ways . . . new friends, fun counselors, endless outdoor activities, and typical summer camp fun like crazy skits and innocent pranks. Pine Cove also offered a peaceful atmosphere, with camp leaders teaching us deep appreciation for the outdoors and for the Bible.

After another full day, I remember us all gathering on the floor of the carpeted mess hall to listen to a special speaker. After some light banter, he began sharing deep from his heart. You could sense his passion as he told us how to invite Jesus into our lives and what it really meant. He said inviting Jesus into our lives was much like inviting someone to move in with us at our house.

When someone comes to *visit* us, we hardly give a thought to how our closets look or what might be hidden in that darkness. In

Choosing Salvation

fact, we sometimes tidy the public areas by tossing things into a closet and closing the door.

When we invite someone to come *live* with us, we are making ourselves more vulnerable. We know there might be an opportunity to develop a much closer relationship to the person we are inviting . . . but we also know they will eventually learn about the junk in our closets.

I invited Jesus to "move in" with me that evening. Somehow I knew He would not be surprised by some of the nasty junk in my closets . . . and He would even help me clean out those dark areas!

Before that summer, I knew about Jesus. That evening at Pine Cove, I actually met Him.

I felt Jesus knocking on the door of my house. When I opened the door and reached out to greet Him with a handshake, He just smiled from ear to ear and pulled me toward Him for a huge warm hug.

Even with all the junk in my closets, I knew He was glad to accept my invitation to move in with me.

But for the next few years I treated Jesus like I treated my parents and my brothers—I was glad to have Him living with me, but I was rather self-centered and preoccupied with my own life.

Although I was usually polite to Jesus and took time to chat periodically, I rarely took time to have many heart-to-heart talks with Him. In fact, I frequently went for long periods without having any meaningful conversation with Him. Sometimes we did things together, but many times I went off to do things on my own. Sometimes I even did things I knew Christ would frown upon.

Still, He was *always* waiting when I came home. He *never left* once He moved in.

As I grew a little older, I realized I didn't know very much about this person I had invited into my house. All my life, I had simply believed what I had been taught, but I never checked matters out for myself.

That's when I decided to get serious about my relationship with Jesus. After lots of research, questions, prayer, and study, I am blessed with a fresh awareness of just how fortunate I am to have Him living in my house.

Still, the best part about this wonderful man I live with is that I know He will *never* move out . . . even when I go through my occasional bouts of fickleness. It's a comfort and peace that cannot be matched.

# Two Words That Changed My Life

by W. Terry Whalin
Scottsdale, Arizona

I slapped the snooze alarm for the third time and finally opened my eyes at Chi Phi, my fraternity house.

Last night had been a late one. After covering an evening speech and interview for the school paper, I worked frantically on the story until just before midnight, when I dropped it into the hands of a waiting editor.

As I struggled out of bed, my mind began turning over the day's schedule. In an hour I had to interview the dean of Indiana University's school of business, then another professor. Oh, yeah—I have a couple of classes to squeeze in, but the assigned reading will have to wait.

Slowly moving through a shower, breakfast, and the bus ride to the newspaper office, I tried to coax my foggy brain to prepare a list of questions for the dean's interview. My life at the *Indiana Daily Student* newspaper revolved around newsprint, wire copy, interviews, and rewriting news releases. Classes were a distinctly secondary reason for attending IU.

After the interviews, I climbed the second-floor steps to the newsroom, hoping I'd be able to meet my 3 P.M. deadline for the campus editor. The clatter of typewriter keys and wire machines along with the room conversation seemed particularly loud. Elbow to elbow, we sat at our yellow desks, pounding away on old manual typewriters, which badly needed to be melted down and replaced with computer terminals.

Hunched over my Royal, I joined eighteen others banging out copy. Maybe it was the noise and rumble around me that frayed my nerves, or my lack of sleep, but I couldn't get my fingers on the right keys. I kept messing up words, then getting mad because I had to backspace and cross them out. I could already hear editor Bruce complaining about how sloppy my copy was.

The harder I tried to concentrate, the worse my typing got. After jamming the keys for the umpteenth time, I could no longer contain my frustration.

"Jesus Christ!" I swore out loud as I unstuck the keys once again, getting ink all over my fingers.

I didn't mean anything serious by my word choice. I used them merely as an expletive, an emotional release. I considered myself a Christian. I went to church with my parents, read the Bible, and even sang in the choir when I went home for breaks. But I was basically following my parents' faith. Christianity didn't mean much to me personally—certainly not enough to worry if I occasionally swore or used the Lord's name in vain.

In the next moment, as I tried once again to focus on my story, a voice interrupted my thoughts.

"Don't say that," the voice said. I looked up and saw a blond woman sitting at another typewriter-equipped desk, apparently working on her own story. Her name was Nancy.

"Someday when you really need Jesus," she continued, "you'll call out but He won't be there." She looked at me with utter seriousness.

Anger roared inside me as she spoke. Who is she to judge me as if she were some authority over me? I fumed.

Then Nancy's face relaxed. "There's a bookstore off campus that sells interesting cards and posters," she said, giving me directions. "You might find some good books about Jesus there."

"I'll have to see," I replied, still angry. Then, knowing I faced a deadline, I turned back to my story. But Nancy's words continued to play in my subconscious. My Christian parents taught me all the basics about faith in God and Jesus Christ, but I felt Christianity was too restrictive. It seemed like little more than a list of things I couldn't do.

College life brought me a sense of freedom from my parents and their faith. Minutes after they left me at my freshman dorm, I bought a pipe. I desperately wanted acceptance from the other students, but I also felt that smoking fit my mental image of a journalist or writer. I choked and sputtered at my first attempts, but continued to draw on the pipe often.

During my first year and a half at college, I immersed myself in journalism and reporting for the *Indiana Daily Student*. My independent lifestyle widened to include joining a fraternity, drinking a lot, and smoking pot.

One Sunday morning I woke up on the couch in a dorm lounge. I couldn't remember anything about the night before except I had been drinking in my fraternity room with a few friends. I frantically searched for my glasses; finally I located them in the nearby rest room.

The memory lapse scared me enough that I considered giving up alcohol. It also made me wonder whether my independence was all it was cracked up to be. But how do I find joy and fulfillment in life? I pondered. As a child, my parents had always taken me to church. But at college, Sunday was my prime time to catch up on sleep and study. Church was nothing more than part of the ritual of going home on breaks.

Strangely, it was during this time of wondering and searching that my encounter with Nancy occurred. The next day I took a walk and located the store Nancy mentioned. At the time, I didn't realize it was a Christian bookstore. Scanning the titles, I came across a book called *Jesus, the Revolutionary*. I wondered how Jesus could have been a revolutionary. So I bought it.

I absorbed the pages of the book. I realized my mental image of Christ consisted of a series of stereotypes—a wimpy figure hanging on the cross or meekly lifting His hand to bless small children. But this book told me Jesus was more than that. He was a friend who would stand by me no matter what the circumstances. He cared intimately about me and loved me enough to die for me. Despite my Christian upbringing, I hadn't given myself the chance to see the full picture of Jesus.

I began to attend several Christian groups on campus and decided to read my Bible. Gradually I found myself losing interest in alcohol, tobacco, and drugs—and wanting to spend more time with other Christians, the Bible, and Jesus. I joined a group called the Christian Student Fellowship, made new friends, and learned a lot in their Bible studies.

I marveled at how far God brought me in a few short years. Certainly He used my parents to lay the groundwork of love and basic understanding about Him. But I had rebelled against their faith.

Actually, the moment of truth for me came that day in the newspaper office, when a courageous Christian woman chose to confront me about two important words that I had spoken all too casually: Jesus Christ.

# allison's concluding thoughts

Dear Reader, I can't leave without asking the most important question: Do you have a personal relationship with the eternal God? I'm not talking about "getting a religion." I'm talking about "getting a relationship." You may have read every word of this book and yet never experienced the peace, strength, and hope our authors have shared with you here.

I spent decades of my life looking for fulfillment in all the wrong places. Today I have peace, strength, and hope because there was a time in my life when I accepted Jesus as my personal Savior. This is what I mean by getting a "relationship," not a "religion."

The way is simple: It only takes three steps.

1. Admit you are a sinner: "For all have sinned and fall short of the glory of God" (Romans 3:23).

2. Believe Jesus is God the Son and He paid the wages of your sin: "For the wages of sin is death [eternal separation from God]; but the gift of God is eternal life in Christ Jesus our Lord" (Romans 6:23).
3. Call upon God: "If thou shalt confess with thy mouth the Lord Jesus, and shalt believe in thine heart that God hath raised him from the dead, thou shalt be saved" (Romans 10:9 KJV).

Our Web site has a "Statement of Faith" page you might find interesting and comforting. On that page you will find helpful (and hopeful) links to other spiritually uplifting Web pages. Please visit us at *www.godallowsuturns.com*.

Salvation is a very personal thing. It is between you and God. I cannot have faith enough for you; no one can. The choice is yours alone. Please know this wonderful gift of hope and healing is available to you. You need only reach out and ask for it. It is never too late to make a U-turn toward God . . . no matter where you have been or what you have done. Remember: The choices we make change the story of our life. Please know I am praying for you.

God's Peace and Protection Always,
Allison Bottke

# about God Allows U-Turns

Along with these exciting new books published by Bethany House Publishers, we want to share with readers the entire scope of the powerful God Allows U-Turns message of hope and healing.

The broad outreach of this organization includes the book you now hold in your hands, as well as other nonfiction and fiction books for adults, youth, and children. Written by Allison Bottke along with other collaborating authors and co-editors, there are currently seventeen books available under the God Allows U-Turns umbrella brand, with additional books releasing soon, including Allison's first novel in the "chick-lit" genre, *A Stitch in Time*, from Bethany House.

Along with books, the God Allows U-Turns outreach also includes tracts, logo merchandise, a line of greeting cards, a speaking ministry, a foundation, and a daily blog. More than fifty thousand copies of the God Allows U-Turns tract, featuring Allison's powerful testimony of making a U-turn toward God, have been distributed around the world. *God Allows U-Turns* anthologies have been translated into Japanese and Portuguese.

Sharing the life-saving message that you can never be so lost or so broken that you can't turn toward God is Allison's main passion in her life and in her ministry.

Visit your local bookstore or the God Allows U-Turns Web site to find out more about this exciting ministry that is helping to change lives: *www.godallowsuturns.com* or write:

Allison Bottke
God Allows U-Turns
PO Box 717
Faribault, MN 55021–0717
editor@godallowsuturns.com

# future volumes of
## *God Allows U-Turns*

The stories you have read in this volume were submitted by readers just like you. From the very start of this inspiring book series, it has been our goal to encourage people from around the world to submit their slice-of-life true short stories for publication.

God Allows U-Turns stories must touch the emotions and stir the heart. We are asking for well-written, personal inspirational pieces showing how faith in God can inspire, encourage, heal, and give hope. We are looking for human-interest stories with a spiritual application, affirming ways in which Christian faith is expressed in the everyday choices of life. We understand that the choices we make change the story of our life.

Our prayer is to publish additional volumes in the U-Turns series every year. Your true story can be from 300 to 1,500 words and must be told with drama, description, and dialogue. Our writer's guidelines are featured on our Web site, and we encourage you to read them carefully. We apologize, but due to the huge response to our request for true stories, we can no longer accept snail-mail submissions. All submissions must be via e-mail or our Web site. Please be advised we cannot respond in any way to the stories submitted. If you wish to know if they have been received, request a "read receipt" at the time of submission. You will only be contacted in the event your story is selected for possible inclusion in a specific volume we are working on.

Fees are paid for stories we publish, and we will be sure to credit you for your submission. Remember, our Web site is filled with up-to-date information about the book project. Additionally, you might want to take advantage of signing up to be on our free eZine list for Internet users. For a list of current *God Allows U-Turns* books open to submissions, as well as related opportunities, visit us at *www.godallowsuturns.com.*

# sharing the success:
# the God Allows U-Turns foundation

One of the most profound lessons in the Bible is giving. The Holy Bible is quite clear in teaching us how we are to live our lives. Scripture refers to this often, and never has the need to share with others been so great.

> Give, and it will be given to you. A good measure, pressed down, shaken together and running over, will be poured into your lap. For with the measure you use, it will be measured to you. (Luke 6:38)

In keeping with the lessons taught us by the Lord our God, we are pleased to have the opportunity to donate a portion of the net profits of every *God Allows U-Turns* book to one or more nonprofit Christian charity. These donations are made through the God

Allows U-Turns Foundation, a funding mechanism established by Kevin and Allison Bottke as a way to share the success of the growing U-Turns outreach ministry.

Additionally, the Strength of Choice Award is also a significant aspect of this vision. Established in 2002, the God Allows U-Turns Strength of Choice Award is given annually at the Golden Scroll Awards banquet sponsored by AWSA—the Advanced Writers and Speakers Association, held just prior to the opening of CBA International.

The God Allows U-Turns Strength of Choice Award goes to the person who in the previous year best exemplified a consistent determination to rise above difficult circumstances while maintaining a clear focus on the One who not only "allows" U-turns, but who remains with us on any life journey, no matter how many twists and turns it may bring. The recipient of this award outwardly lives Philippians 4:12–13: "I know what it is to be in need, and I know what it is to have plenty. I have learned the secret of being content in any and every situation, whether well fed or hungry, whether living in plenty or in want. I can do everything through him who gives me strength." Past recipients have been Gene and Carol Kent, Ramona Richards, and Dan Penwell.

For more details visit the Web site at *www.godallowsuturns.com*.

# about the authors

ALLISON BOTTKE lives in southern Minnesota on a twenty-five-acre hobby farm with her entrepreneur husband, Kevin. She is a relatively "new" Christian, coming to the fold in 1989 as a result of a dramatic life U-turn. The driving force behind God Allows U-Turns, she has a growing passion to share with others the healing and hope offered by the Lord Jesus Christ. Allison has a wonderful ability to inspire and encourage audiences with her down-to-earth speaking style as she relates her personal testimony of how God orchestrated a dramatic U-turn in her life. Lovingly dubbed "The U-Turns Poster Girl," you can find out more about Allison by visiting her information page on the book's Web site: *www.godallowsuturns.com/aboutauthor.htm*.

CHERYLL HUTCHINGS has been a Christian since the age of twelve and has always let God lead her in life. The best adventure He's led her on so far has been joining the God Allows U-Turns project on the ground floor of the ministry when it began in 2000. Married to Bob for twenty-eight years, they have a twenty-three-year-old son named Aaron, who is working full time in the computer industry, and a twenty-year-old son named Scott, who is a corporal in the United States Marine Corps. They live in the country in a rambling ranch in Medina, Ohio, which sits on several acres of peaceful seclusion, surrounded by the Lord's beautiful nature and wildlife.

# about our web site

We first announced God Allows U-Turns on the World Wide Web in February of 2000. The Lord used this avenue of communication to reach across all borders: geographic as well as racial, political, denominational, and social. Stories began to come to us via our Web site, first by the dozens, then hundreds, and now thousands.

While our Web site is specific to the God Allows U-Turns book series, you will find we also offer important links to other major Christian Web sites, links we encourage you to visit. Additionally, we have placed a "Statement of Faith" page on our site to clearly establish our beliefs. Also of note is the page "How to Be Born Again" (*www.godallowsuturns.com/stmtfaith.htm*). This section on our Web site is visited by thousands of people every year.

The global opportunities a Web site provides are mind-boggling, but we need your help to make the kind of impact we know is possible. Please visit our Web site and forward it to your family and friends. Virtually everyone has a story to tell, and future volumes will enable those stories to be told. We are accepting true short stories now for future volumes. Visit our "Future Volumes" page on our Web site to find out more.

Remember, our Web site is filled with up-to-date information about the book project. You will be able to access tour and book-signing calendars on the site, as well as read stories from the current volume. Additionally, you might want to take advantage of signing up for our free eZine list for Internet users. Don't miss out on current news and reviews. We invite you to visit our daily blog at *www.godallowsuturns.blogspot.com.*

# about our contributors

**Genetta Adair** enjoyed meeting with Missy Mitchell, listening to her music, and corresponding with her. Genetta writes from her rural home near Memphis, Tennessee, with Bella, her yellow Labrador, by her side.

**Eva M. Allen** is currently a full-time mom and a part-time muralist. When not tending to her two boys or painting various artistic expressions, she might be gardening, guitar-playing, going to garage sales—-or making cheesecake.

**Nancy C. Anderson** (*www.NancyCAnderson.com*) is an award-winning author, columnist for Crosswalk.com, and a contributing writer for many teen books, including *Chicken Soup for the Father & Daughter Soul*, *God's Way for Teens*, *Stuff a Girl's Gotta Know*, and *Beauty Is Soul Deep*.

**Esther M. Bailey** is the author of *God's Little Messengers* and *Voices of God*. Living in Scottsdale, Arizona, Bailey enjoys dining out with friends and sharing the good news of Jesus Christ with those who need Him. E-mail baileywick@juno.com (*www.baileywick.net*).

**Mary Lee Brown** has been writing stories for children and teens since the writing bug hit her several years ago, and she has two novels "ready to go." Because she loves hearing others tell stories, she started a memoir writing business: Down Memory Lane. Contact Mary at *mary@tscwa.com*.

**Sandra J. Campbell** is a published author residing in Garden City, Michigan. She is delighted to be one of ThreeOlBags, a trio of travel writers who collaborate on articles about people and places of interest in their Great Lake State and beyond! Contact Sandra at *www.threeolbags.com*.

**Christy Carlson** resides in Florida with her husband of five years, Jonathan, and their daughter, Paisley. She met Christ when she was ten years old and has been following Him ever since. Her hobbies include photography, scrapbooking, writing, reading, camping, and other outdoor activities.

**Candace Carteen** resides in both Battle Ground and Ocean Park, Washington. She lives with her best friend/husband, George, and her adopted son, Keefer. She's a member of ToastMasters International and does speaking engagements throughout the Northwest. Contact her at scribecandace@netzero.net or at PO Box 635 in Ocean Park, WA 98640.

**Kitty Chappell** is an award-winning author, a luncheon and retreat speaker, and has made television and radio appearances. She lives in Gilbert, Arizona. For information about her book, *Sins of a*

*Father, Forgiving the Unforgivable* (New Hope Publishers, 2003), currently being made into a movie, visit *www.KittyChappell.com* or e-mail her at kittchap@cox.net.

**Joan Clayton** writes from her home in New Mexico. She and her husband, Emmitt, are retired educators. Joan has authored seven books and is the religion columnist for her local newspaper. Visit her Web site at *www.joanclayton.com* or e-mail her at joan@jucca.net.

**Ann Jean Czerwinski** is the Educational Services Manager at WQLN-TV in Erie, Pennsylvania. She has a passion for writing about special people who have touched her life. Ann Jean and her husband, Doug, have three children: Joshua, Jason, and Jessica. E-mail her at ajczerwinski@adelphia.net.

**Jennifer Devlin** is a retired Army wife and women's ministry leader with a vibrant speaking, writing, and teaching ministry. She is blessed with a wonderful husband and son, and resides in northern Alabama. Please visit her Web site *www.ministryforlife.com* or e-mail her at jennifer@ministryforlife.com for more details.

**Gail Dickert** graduated from Cincinnati Christian University and has been involved with youth ministry since 1997. Gail dedicates "Kay's" story to the courageous teenagers she met while serving as a youth director and girls' volleyball coach in Newport, Kentucky. Visit her at *www.authorhouse.com* or e-mail her at gluvsvegas@yahoo.com.

**Wendy Dunham** is a mother of two wonderful children, a registered therapist for differently abled students, and an inspirational writer. She can be reached at wendydunham@bluefrog.com.

**Sharon Dunn** is the author of the *Ruby Taylor* mysteries. Book

Two, *Sassy Cinderella and the Valiant Vigilante,* was voted Book of the Year by American Christian Fiction Writers. She lives in Montana with her husband and three children. Read more about Sharon at *www.sharondunnbooks.com* or e-mail her at sdunn@int.net.

**Ann Eide,** a freelance writer/author, is a devoted wife and stay-at-home mom. She incorporates daily experiences into the articles and daily devotionals she writes. Ann believes the best way to witness for Christ is to always be true to one's self. Visit *www.theardentpen.com* or e-mail her at AnnE02@cableone.net.

**Laura Farrar** is a high school student from the California Bay Area. She loves writing, reading, music, gymnastics, scrapbooking, youth group, and animals. Her poems and stories have been published in several magazines and eZines. She can be reached by e-mail at LFwrites@yahoo.com.

**Lynette Marie Galisewski** would not be considered shy today, but that is only because God has continued to make her brave! A counselor, teacher, writer, competitive body builder, and horse lover, Lynette loves to live on her frontiers . . . keeping up with her two teenage kids!

**Carol Genengels'** stories have appeared in *Reminisce, Stories for the Spirit-Filled Believer, God Allows U-Turns, Chicken Soup for the Soul, God Answers Mom's Prayers,* and *Journeys of Friendship.* Her book *Unfailing Love* details Carol's life story. E-mail her at awtcarolg@aol.com.

**Nancy B. Gibbs** is a pastor's wife, author of four books, and motivational speaker. Nancy writes two weekly newspaper columns and has contributed to numerous magazines, devotional guides, and anthologies. Nancy may be reached by e-mail, Daiseydood@aol.com or through her Web site at *www.nancybgibbs.com*.

**Charles Gibson** lives in Centerville, Minnesota, with his wife, Tricia, and little boy, Trenton. He works as a full-time technical writer and part-time freelance writer. He was published in the *God Allows U-Turns: American Moments* volume. Contact him at ctgibson@usfamily.net or visit his Web site at *www.chadgibson.blogspot.com*.

**Rebekah Hamrick** is the editor of *Teen Light,* a totally teen-authored Christian magazine, and moderates its online teen-to-teen support group. Her writing has appeared in a variety of anthologies and magazines, including Focus on the Family. She can be reached through *Teen Light*'s Web site, *www.teenlight.org*.

**Tyrice Harrell** was born and raised in Brooklyn, New York, and currently lives in New York City. He is a freelance writer, songwriter, and musician. He is an alumnus of both John and Wales University and Sunny Old Westbury. E-mail him at tyriceharrell@hotmail.com.

**Christy Heitger Casbon,** a regular contributing writer to several Christian teen magazines, also writes about pet health, cabin living, and parenting. She's published hundreds of magazine articles. Her work is also in *Chicken Soup for the Christian Teenage Soul.* Christy lives in Noblesville, Indiana. E-mail her at christy_heitger_casbon@insightbb.com.

**D. Marie Hutko** is a freelance writer whose writing credits include magazine, newspaper, and online publications such as *Baltimore's Child, The Montgomery Journal, Towne,* and *Now What?* She is making her book debut in *The Choices Teens Make* with a story closest to her heart. Visit her at *http://hometown.aol.com/ rhiannon773/myhomepage/business.html* or e-mail her at Rhiannon773@aol.com.

**Jan Kern** is an author and speaker who is currently working on a nonfiction book about self-injury. She and her husband have been a part of residential ministry for at-risk youth for more than twenty years. Write her at kernjan@hotmail.com or visit *www.jankern.com.*

**Candice Killion** has recently contributed to *Chicken Soup for the Healthy Living Soul: Menopause* and the *Our Fathers Who Art In Heaven* project; she is also the recipient of the 2005 Chistell Prize for Poetry. Visit *www.candykillion.com* or e-mail candykillion@bellsouth.net.

**Karen Kosman** is a wife, mother, grandmother, inspirational speaker, and freelance writer. Karen's joy and zest for life warms hearts. She has authored stories in compilation books and magazine articles. Her latest article, "Finding Freedom," appeared in *Power for Living, 2005.* Contact her at ComKosman@aol.com or *www.renewalofhope.com.*

**Helen Grace Lescheid**, storyteller of hope and motivational speaker, has authored three books: *Lead Kindly Light, Treasures of Darkness,* and *You Raised Me Up.* She has had numerous articles published in *Reader's Digest, Guideposts,* and other magazines. She is the mother of five and grandmother of three.

**Lynn Ludwick**, mother of four, grandmother of six, lives in a small town with her husband and one-eyed cat. Family, church, friends, quilting, gardening, and writing occupy her time. Her monthly column, "Looking at Life," appears in *The Christian Journal.* She is writing her first novel.

**Steven Manchester**, the father of three beautiful children, is the published author of *The Rockin' Chair, The Unexpected Storm, A Father's Love,* and *Jacob Evans,* as well as several books under the pseudonym Steven Herberts. Three of his screenplays have been produced as films. See: *www.StevenManchester.com* or e-mail him at info@StevenManchester.com.

**Sandra McGarrity** lives in Chesapeake, Virginia. Her stories have appeared in previous U-Turns volumes. Visit her Web page at *www.heartwarmers4u.com/members?woody* or e-mail her at mygr8m8@aol.com.

**Amber Renee Medrano** is wife to David and mother to Nathaniel and Shane. In the midst of many life storms, God has preserved and blessed her family through His abundant grace. You can read more about the Medrano family by visiting their Web site: *www.shanesnotebook.com* or e-mail her at amber.medrano@cox.net.

**Michele Newhouse** lives in Edmond, Oklahoma, with her husband and teenage son. Additional stories of how Christ has touched Michele's life are available online at *www.covenantpro.com,* e-mail newhouse@covenantpro.com, or by calling Michele at 405–396–3321.

**Laura Nixon** is a seventeen-year-old high school senior living in Ohio. Upon graduation, she plans on attending Olivet Nazarene University.

**Carol Oyanagi** is a writer living in Minnesota with her husband. Her published works include articles, poetry, short stories, and drama sketches. She leads a Christian dance troupe called Ransomed Messengers and enjoys biking, reading, theatre, skiing, cooking, and long walks. E-mail her at coyanagi@aol.com.

**Jeanne Pallos** is the author of several published stories for adults and children, and she is a board member of The Orange County Christian Writers Fellowship. She and her husband live in Laguna Niguel, California, and are the proud parents of two adult children. You can e-mail her at jlpallos@cox.net.

**Cara Symank Parker**, coauthor of *The Mother-Daughter Legacy* by Regal Books (written with her grandmother Carole Lewis), is a graduate of Texas A&M University. She resides in Abilene, Texas, with husband, Michael, who is majoring in Youth Ministry Education at Hardin-Simmons University. Her desire is to spread the love of Christ to others around her.

**Michael T. Powers**, a youth pastor, resides in Wisconsin with his wife, Kristi, and their three boys. His stories appear in twenty-three different inspirational books including his own, entitled *Heart Touchers*. To join the thousands of worldwide readers on his inspirational e-mail list visit: *www.Heart4Teens.com* or e-mail: Heart4Teens@aol.com.

**Carolyn Byers Ruch** is a mother to four amazing teenagers and part-time mother to their hungry friends. When she is not writing about sexual abuse and pornography, she makes frequent trips to Costco for junk food. E-mail her at undeserveddisgrace@comcast.net.

**Bonnie Scheid**, following a teaching career, writes on Christian themes, leads a Senior Stretch Group each morning, contributes time to PEO (a Philanthropic Educational Christian Organization), and serves as deacon at St. James Presbyterian Church. She and her husband keep in touch with six grown children and nine grandchildren across the U.S.

**Linda Evans Shepherd**, coauthor of *The Pot Luck Club*, is a national radio host and president of the Right of the Heart Ministries. She's the founder and director of Advanced Writers and Speakers Association. To contact Linda see *www.InspiredSpeakers.com*.

**Laura L. Smith** is the author of the children's book *Cantaloupe Trees*, as well as stories in the *God Allows U-Turns, Chicken Soup for the Soul*, and *God's Way* anthologies. She graduated from Miami University and lives with her husband and children in Oxford, Ohio. E-mail her at reds@mindspring.com.

**Gloria Cassity Stargel**, a writer for *Guideposts*, among other publications, has written an award-winning book called *The Healing: One Family's Victorious Struggle With Cancer*, which answers the question, "Does God still heal today?" Check out her Web site at *www.brightmorning.com*.

**Joyce Stark** was born and lives in northeast Scotland. She works part time for the Community Mental Health Board and part time as a freelance writer. She loves to travel and meet people from different cultures and then go home and write about them.

**Heather Tomasello** lives in Virginia with her husband and two children. A freelance writer, she's a popular speaker for schools, libraries, and writers' groups, and she is the author of two books for young adults, including *Before You Call Mom: A Real World Survival Guide*. Visit her at *www.heathertomasello.com*.

**Shelley Wake** is the author of nine nonfiction titles, three children's books, and numerous articles and essays. She has degrees in business and science and a Master of Arts in Professional Writing. She also owns and operates the Writing Stuff Web site. E-mail her at shelleywake@ozemail.com.au or check out her Web site at *www.writingstuff.com*.

**Amy Nicole Wallace** is a wife, mom of three amazing daughters, and writer, living in Atlanta, Georgia. She leads an awesome youth discipleship group and young ladies' Sunday morning Bible study. Her recent credits include contributing author in *God Answers Mom's Prayers*. Visit her at *http://peek-a-booicu.blogspot.com*.

**Sharen Watson** currently resides in Highlands Ranch, Colorado. Married twenty-five years to Ray, they have one daughter, a son-in-law, two sons, and one spoiled Lhasa Apso, Gia. Sharen is a speaker, author, and founder of Words for the Journey Christian Writer's Guild. Please visit *www.wordsforthejourney.org* or e-mail her at IRite4Him@aol.com.

**W. Terry Whalin** lives in Scottsdale, Arizona, and has written for more than fifty magazines and more than sixty books, including his latest, *Book Proposals That $ell: 21 Secrets to Speed Your Success*. He also created a popular site for writers, *www.rightwriting.com*.

**Sydney Tate Williams** is a tenth-grade honor roll student at Sikeston Senior High School and lives in Sikeston, Missouri, with her parents. Tate is an active member of her church youth group, 4H Rodeo, and Fellowship of Christian Athletes. She is the president of the Green Peppers Pep Club, editor of the yearbook, and serves as president of her school newspaper staff.